Cahaba Prison
and the
Sultana Disaster

Cahaba Prison

and the

Sultana Disaster

William O. Bryant

The University of Alabama Press
Tuscaloosa and London

Copyright © 1990 by
The University of Alabama Press
Tuscaloosa, Alabama 35487–0380
All rights reserved
Manufactured in the United States of America

∞

The paper on which this book is printed
meets the minimum requirements of
American National Standard for
Information Science-Permanence of Paper for
Printed Library Materials,
ANSI A39.48–1984.

Library of Congress Cataloging-in-Publication Data

Bryant, William O.
    Cahaba Prison and the Sultana disaster / William O. Bryant.
        p.   cm.
    Bibliography: p.
    Includes index.
    ISBN 0-8173-0468-1 (alk. paper)
    1. Cahaba Federal Prison (Cahaba, Ala.)   2. Cahaba (Ala.)—
History.   3. United States—History—Civil War, 1861–1865—
Prisoners and prisons.   4. Sultana (Steamboat)   5. Steamboat
disasters—Mississippi River—History—19th century.   I. Title.
E612.C2B77   1990
973.7'71—dc20   89-33833
                                                                    CIP

British Library Cataloguing-in-Publication Data available

This is for
Frank L. Owsley, Jr., and
Joseph H. Harrison, Jr.;
for my parents;
and for my wife, Travis.

Contents

ACKNOWLEDGMENTS

The following made contributions that are
valued highly: Thomas A. Belser, Jr.;
Robin F. A. Fabel; and J. Wayne Flynt;
Linda Derry of the Old Cahawba Preservation Project;
H. David Williams;
Gene A. Smith; and James B. Segrest.

Cahaba Prison
and the
Sultana Disaster

The Selma-Cahaba-Demopolis area during the Civil War

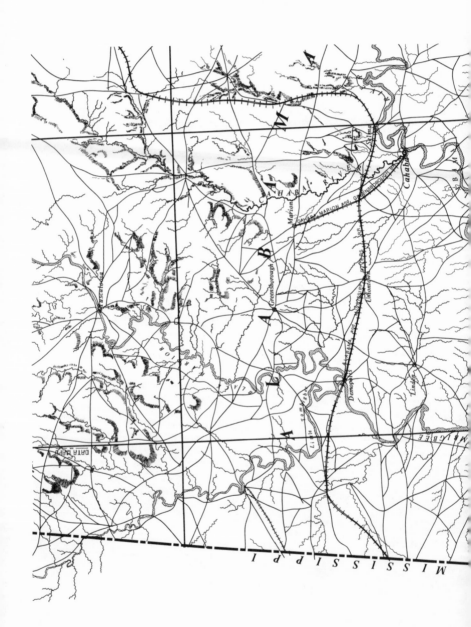

1
The Civil War and
Its Prisons

In the quiet Alabama backwater of the Civil War, the Confederate government operated a major prison camp for Union captives. It was at Cahaba, a place formerly of much importance, but also of much adversity. The state's first capital, Cahaba was about ten miles south of Selma at the junction of the Cahaba and Alabama rivers. The prison, on the Alabama's bank, was established in the spring or summer of 1863—the record is inexact. Authorities ordered it closed six to nine months later and sent the captives to the newer and much bigger prison at Andersonville, Georgia. Cahaba Federal Prison, its official name, nevertheless remained a collecting station for men en route to Andersonville and was reestablished as a regular facility when Andersonville overflowed with men and the South became most desperate for everything, including places to keep captured Federal soldiers. Only nine months of war remained when the South made the prison permanent, or as permanent as a dying Confederacy could make anything.

1

The prison was a warehouse intended for agricultural products; not an old warehouse fallen into disuse as the prisoners thought, but a new and unfinished one. Although it covered less than one-third acre, more people lived there than lived in the entire town, and at night each man barely had room to lie down.

After the war, the prison and what happened there faded into historic inattention relieved only by occasional mention or a rediscovered memoir pleading for notice. It was not certain even where the prison stood. The building was torn down several years after the war; the town perished and people quickly forgot.

Cahaba Federal Prison, or Castle Morgan as it was known unofficially, likely was the most overcrowded of all such Civil War camps, North or South. It was the scene of a rare attempt at a mass breakout and the murder of a prisoner in retaliation. The rivers flooded the warehouse, and men sought dry havens for days in the rafters or on piles of wood and debris. The prison also was a place of much human kindness.

About five thousand men were Cahaba inmates. A thousand or more of them died after release back into the supposed safety of their own army. They were crowded aboard the steamboat *Sultana* for shipment home, and it blew up and burned in the Mississippi River. The disaster was the worst ever to involve any vessel flying the U.S. flag, in peace or war, a disaster of such proportions one turns to the *Titanic* for comparison in loss and drama.

It is provable that no Confederate officer or official at Cahaba or in Richmond, save one, intended harm to any federal soldier held at the prison. The exception, Lieutenant Colonel Sam Jones, commander of the post at Cahaba, came to power by chance, and those running the southern prisoner of war system knew nothing of him. They chose Captain H. A. M. Henderson to command the prison. He achieved the near impossible: he was a prison keeper much admired by the men imprisoned.

Unfortunately for the men, Henderson and Jones shared authority. Jones, who commanded the guards, also took charge of the prison and its inmates when Henderson was away on his other duties as an assistant agent for the exchange of prisoners. Henderson enjoyed a postwar life of considerable accomplishment, prestige, and honor. Jones disappeared. Otherwise, poor Henry Wirz, the commander at Andersonville, might have escaped the ignominy of being the only man executed after the conflict for war crimes.

A few of the inmates claimed Cahaba was as bad as Andersonville. The records show it was not. The food probably was about the same at both, and the Cahaba men had less space. But sanitation and medical care at Cahaba were as good as was then possible, and the waves of death in the Georgia prison were absent in the Alabama one. The death rate at Cahaba was less than 5 percent, making it a relatively safe place for soldiers to be in time of war. Taken with the *Sultana* tragedy, however, Cahaba becomes important for a reason other than demonstrating that southern prisons were not all excessively deadly or prison commanders always incompetent. Despite the unusually low death rate, so many of its inmates never saw home and family again because of the *Sultana* tragedy that an Andersonville man had a better chance of getting back than did a Cahaba man.

Cahaba Federal Prison, like the numerous other prison camps North and South, resulted from one of the many unexpected circumstances forced on unprepared officials by a war of surprising scope and ferocity. The Civil War may provide the purest example of the axiom that war is one of the most difficult of human activities for which to prepare. None is like the one before, which provided the latest experience, and in this one the conflict's nature compounded the problem profoundly. It was impossible for a nation such as the United States of the mid-nineteenth century, with political power shared about equally between the contending sides, truly to ready itself to divide and fight. North and South, therefore, began the war without adequate means and experience, equipped only with causes both sides thought noble enough to merit noble effort. Men had to learn as they went and so made terrible mistakes at terrible cost in blood and treasure. Both sides were strained enormously from the first as the war became bigger and bloodier than most people imagined possible.

The United States Army of regulars in 1861, just before the first shots, included only 13,024 men and officers, most of them scattered in frontier posts and coastal forts. These numbers were more than equaled on the casualty lists of some battles in the killing that followed. That is almost exactly the total of Confederate casualties at Chancellorsville, the casualties of one side. About that many men died while imprisoned at Andersonville; more than three times as many were killed, wounded, or were missing when the shooting stopped at Gettysburg.[1]

If the North was ill-prepared with such a small army, the South was woefully more so, having no army at all and no government. The South also had to attempt instant fashioning of both and all that both needed while strangling on a blockade of its ports by the Union navy. Too, the South's white population, from which it drew its soldiery, was less than a third of the North's, while the Union recruited both whites and blacks, and recruited widely in Europe. For ready troops the South had scattered organizations of state militia, indifferently trained, led, and equipped, but so did the North. While both sides had unschooled volunteers by the hundred thousand, the South at first had few weapons with which to equip them. It obtained the training and experience of 182 U.S. officers of the rank of brigadier general or higher who decided to lead southern instead of northern troops, but it had no organization for an army and little manufacturing of the goods an army must have.[2]

Figures used by historians James G. Randall and David Herbert Donald show the industrial disparity. The North had 110,000 manufacturing *plants* at war's start, and the South 110,000 manufacturing *workers*. Furthermore, there was not much in the way of a transportation system to get the things the South needed from place to place even when supplies were available. Never were there enough horses and mules, many of the rivers ran the wrong way—away from the fighting fronts—and the railroads were a hodge-podge of lines operating on rails of differing gauges, impossible to make into a unified system. In this first big war in which railroads played a major part by the swift movement of troops and supplies, track repairs or extensions in the Confederacy could be made only by tearing up one road to provide rails for another. The South did not manufacture a single bar of railroad iron during the entire war, and portions of some lines carried trains on wooden rails topped with thin straps of iron.[3]

As an example of the difficulties, shipping supplies from Meridian, Mississippi, to Atlanta involved loading at Meridian for a short rail trip to the Tombigbee River in Alabama. At McDowell's Bluff, the freight was unloaded and carried by ferry across the river to Demopolis where it was reloaded onto the cars of the Alabama and Mississippi Rivers Railroad for the run to Selma. It was then unloaded again to be carried by steamboat the forty miles to Montgomery, since the Alabama River was the Selma-Montgomery connection. At Montgomery, the supplies were shifted to the cars of the Montgomery and West Point Railroad. At the Georgia border, they were unloaded and

The Civil War and Its Prisons   5

reloaded onto yet another train because the connecting Atlanta and West Point had tracks and equipment of a wider gauge than the line from Montgomery. For part of the war this Meridian-Atlanta route was a main segment of the only major trans-South rail artery, and the difficulties described were those prevailing at its greatest efficiency.[4]

Examples of southern privation are countless. The horses of General R. E. Lee's Army of Northern Virginia, their health nearly as essential as that of soldiers, wintered on the bark of trees for want of fodder. General James Longstreet left some of his already scarce artillery in Virginia when he led his corps to Chickamauga because he had too few horses to pull the guns.[5]

Conditions steadily worsened as the Union took precious southern territory and the blockade became more expert with experience and new ships. The South's overseas commerce shriveled. Cotton, the fuel that once ran the South, provided only a cold fire if not sent to Europe and exchanged for arms, medicine, and other goods sorely needed and otherwise not obtainable. The Confederacy came to be virtually without means. In Richmond in May 1864, shortly before Cahaba Federal Prison was made permanent, flour sold for 275 dollars a barrel, potatoes twenty-five dollars a bushel, and bacon nine dollars a pound. Quinine, a fever-reducing and antimalarial drug used also for everything from diarrhea to syphilis, sold for 188 dollars an ounce on the open market. Samuel Preston Moore, the Confederate army's surgeon general, recommended a substitute made from whiskey and the bark of dogwood, poplar, and willow trees. Some sources say it was unsatisfactory, but it probably relieved mild pain and reduced fever. Other medicinal alternatives included cucumbers for burns, charcoal for diphtheria, and geranium for diarrhea. In Cahaba, the price of coffee rose to seventy dollars a pound. Women created a substitute from okra seed parched and ground, or from sweet potatoes, and brewed the best "tea" from black raspberry vines.[6]

In another famous example of southern want, General Lee once had guests to whom he could serve only his own usual midday fare of cabbage boiled with a little salt, but this time flavored with a bit of bacon. The meat was so scant, however, the embarrassed guests declined to eat it. The bacon, moreover, was borrowed, there being none in camp, and when the guests passed it by, Lee returned it to the owner.[7]

Some things improved for a time during the war. The South managed to find arms for its volunteers and to manufacture sufficient ammunition. In some areas it grew plenty of food, as General William T. Sherman's troops discovered on their march from Atlanta to the sea, but it could not get much of it to the right places for want of transportation.

Southern troops went hungry and marched and fought in bare feet. Many slept through winter nights without blankets. When little could be found even for their horses, without which supplies, artillery, and ambulance wagons could not be moved or sufficient cavalry put in the field, and when the foremost general could not find food for important guests, it may be understandable that captured Union soldiers knew severe privation that too often resulted in death. If prisoners at Cahaba and other similar stations in the South were hungry, so were soldiers in the Confederate ranks. The Army of Tennessee awaited the end of the winter of 1863–1864 and the coming of Sherman on a diet of cornbread and sweet potatoes or cornbread and peanuts. Meat arrived no more than three times a week.[8]

Late in the war, Doctor Joseph Jones, professor of medical chemistry at the Medical College of Georgia in Augusta, obtained the permission of Surgeon General Moore to visit

Andersonville and investigate the nature of the diseases ravaging the prison. The war ended before he finished his report,[9] but it includes an excellent statement of the problems faced by the South and its prisoners.

As long as the Confederate Government is compelled to hold these prisoners as hostages for the safe exchange of the captive men of its own armies, it is difficult to see how the sufferings of such an immense army of prisoners, equal in numbers at least to one-fourth of the Confederate forces actively engaged in the field, can to any extent be mitigated in a purely agricultural country, sparsely settled, with imperfect lines of communication, with an inflated and almost worthless currency, with no commerce, with few or no manufactories of importance, cut off from all communication with the surrounding world, and deprived of even the necessary medicines, which have been declared "contraband of war" by the hostile government. With torn and bleeding borders, with constantly diminishing powers of subsistence and resistance, with its entire fighting population in arms, with a constant retreat of the armies and population upon the central portions of the country, and with corresponding demands upon the supplies of the overcrowded interior, and with corresponding increase of travel upon the dilapidated railroads, the maintenance of the prisoners becomes every day more difficult and onerous.[10]

For an army to keep large numbers of prisoners was unusual in that day, and men did not have the experience for it anymore than they had the experience for fighting on such a huge scale. The civilized way was to give prisoners back to their own people, to free them on parole and on their honor not to fight again until exchanged, and then to swap them on something approaching a man-for-man basis. A captured private was released on parole and later traded for a private of the other side, the exchange being largely a matter of paperwork. Or several privates sufficed for the exchange of one officer. It was quite complicated and the record-keeping enormous.

The exchange system operated only haltingly, and both sides had to keep prisoners. Trouble arose from the beginning, including Union reluctance to negotiate exchanges with a Confederacy it could not recognize as a separate entity for political and diplomatic reasons. Hostages were held on both sides amid threats of executions and retaliation. Paroled men went back on duty before exchange and rejoined the fighting while still officially prisoners. The Union claimed that its men often returned from captivity in poor physical shape, starved and unfit for duty, in much worse condition than the captives it returned to the South.

There also was the considerable problem of freed soldiers insisting on a furlough and refusing any duty before receiving one. This led to the suspicion that some men purposely surrendered in the belief that they would be exchanged quickly and that regulations required the army then to compensate them for their captivity with a vacation. The problem arose also of what to do with captured black soldiers, often escaped slaves. The North insisted they be treated like other Union men, but the Confederacy denied they were eligible for parole or exchange and sent them back to their owners or employed them as laborers.[11]

When U. S. Grant became lieutenant general in command of all Union armies, he looked realistically at the matter and decided it was better to keep southern men than to release them and have to fight them again. Many Confederates were in a revolving door. They fought and were captured. They were paroled and exchanged. Then they soon were back in the lines to fight yet again. Writing to Major General Benjamin F. Butler, commissioner of prisoner exchange, Grant said on August 18, 1864, "If we commence a system of exchange which liberates all prisoners taken, we will have to fight on until the whole South is exterminated." Every released southerner, he said, "becomes an active soldier against us at once either directly or indirectly," but, "if we hold those caught they amount to no more than dead men."

"It is hard on our men held in Southern prisons not to exchange them, but it is humanity to those left in the ranks to fight our battles," Grant said.[12]

The following day, he wrote to Secretary of State William H. Seward, "We ought not to make a single exchange nor release a prisoner on any pretext whatever until the war closes. We have got to fight until the military power of the South is exhausted, and if we release or exchange prisoners captured it simply becomes a war of extermination."[13]

Exchanges continued only rarely during the last months, until just before the end, and usually were permitted only in selected cases such as captured civilians or soldiers unfit for further duty. Men North and South thus had to suffer enormously.

On both sides caring for prisoners was of low priority compared with other needs. They were an added burden with the burden already too heavy—an unwanted increase in population without an increase in resources, and with the additional difficulty of the increase being largely unproductive and most unpopular.

Much more than that was to blame for the plight of prisoners, however. Human clumsiness was greatly involved, and just to be in the army was hazardous. Disease and malnutrition killed many more soldiers in the 1860s than did weapons. Knowledge of medicine, sanitation, and nutrition was primitive. Soldiers died of scurvy while in quiet camps and receiving the best their government could provide. A diet lacking vitamin C, provided by fruit and leafy vegetables, is the sole cause of scurvy. Therefore, men under the care of their own authorities sickened on a regular ration of crackers and beef or pork, even if abundantly provided.

The Sixty-fifth U.S. Colored Infantry is the premier example of what could happen. Recruited throughout Missouri, its members reported to Benton Barracks in that state in the winter of 1863 before being equipped by the military. All were thinly clad, many without shoes or hats. The ravages of exposure and the resulting diseases led to many amputations of feet and hands, and 755 deaths, none involving combat. A look at the losses of the twenty Union regiments that suffered the largest number of deaths from noncombat causes shows nearly 9,000 such victims, while the same units had 1,317 killed or mortally wounded in battle. This means only about 1 in 7 of the deaths in these units resulted from enemy action.[14]

It is not surprising, then, that prisoners died in large numbers in many places on both sides, since they were last in line for supplies and food, and circumstances kept them in places where elementary sanitation was difficult and all sorts of vermin abundant. Too, they were limited to the food and clothing provided or that they could bribe from guards. The soldier outside a prison stockade at least had the freedom to forage for warm clothes and a better diet.

The War Department compiled figures in 1866 that showed the North held 220,000 Confederate prisoners and the South 126,000 Union men. Of these, the government said, 26,436 southerners died in northern camps and 22,576 Federals died in southern camps. James Ford Rhodes, a northern historian, studied the records forty years later and determined that the South held more Union men than the government reported, 194,000, while the Union held fewer Confederates, 215,000. But he said the government's totals on deaths substantially were correct. Rhodes's figures, arrived at some distance from the passions and prejudices of the war, appear more accurate, and notable historians such as William Best Hesseltine and Bruce Catton accepted them. These figures make the death rates of a little more than 12 percent in the North and 15.5 percent in the South too close for one side to accuse the other. Although southerners may maintain with considerable justification that the North had less excuse because of its much more abundant resources, prison camps of one side were about as deadly as those of the other.[15]

Cahaba Federal Prison is an important part of the prison history of the Civil War. It was exceptional because of its low death rate and because of unique events that occurred there or began there. Yet it is little known. Hesseltine gave it but part of one sentence in his *Civil War Prisons: A Study in War Psychology*,[16] observing only that it was closed early in 1864. He did not mention its later use.

It received a hundred words in the lengthy section on prisons in the ten-volume basic and primary *Photographic History of the Civil War*. It also has been the subject of at least one magazine article, and an article in a historical quarterly.[17]

Of the Cahaba survivors, only Private Jesse Hawes left a lengthy published memoir.[18] Two others published brief narratives of their experiences both at Cahaba and on the *Sultana*, and one included Cahaba in a book on his total war experiences. The slim accounts of at least three other men are provided in other books or articles on the war or prisons. But nothing of significance has been published since Hawes's *Cahaba: A Story of Captive Boys in Blue* appeared in 1888.

All such prison stories must be regarded suspiciously, since the authors were intimately involved, many saw themselves as victims of deliberate cruelty, and many sought to prove claims for pensions. But by comparing Hawes's work with available records and the memoirs of

Jesse Hawes as he appeared in his own book (Jesse Hawes, *Cahaba: A Story of Captive Boys in Blue*)

The Civil War and Its Prisons 13

others, he can be shown to be accurate in much of the detail about which he wrote. Hesseltine, who otherwise paid scant attention to Cahaba, included a footnote in which he called Hawes's book, "an excellent account of this prison, from the standpoint of an inmate." Hawes had faults, however. He relied sometimes on secondhand reports and rumors, and he was zealous in trying to depict Cahaba as the equal in misery of Andersonville. "Cahaba was even worse," he said. Lewis W. Day, who wrote the history of the 101st Ohio Infantry, wrote, however, "This was one of the exceedingly well-conducted prisons in the whole South." The Federal general who received the exchanged Cahaba men near the end of the war, along with a group from Andersonville, also would have disagreed with Hawes. He reported many of the prisoners in excellent health, "the Cahaba prisoners particularly."[19]

The relative lack of attention to Cahaba is explainable on several points. Cahaba Federal Prison, only one of many such places, was much smaller than Andersonville and apparently produced few complaints. But, of course, the death of so many Cahaba men on the Mississippi in the explosion and sinking of the *Sultana* sadly reduced the potential for both complaints and memoirs.

Much of the detail of what happened on the *Sultana* is known because of Chester D. Berry's *Loss of the Sultana and Reminiscences of Survivors*. Berry, a passenger on the boat, attended a reunion of survivors and collected many personal accounts of the tragedy, which he published twenty-seven years after the accident. One modern full-length study is available, James Elliott's excellent *Transport to Disaster*.[20] However, the disaster remains the subject of occasional journal and newspaper articles 125 years after it occurred.

The *Sultana* horror received remarkably little attention at the time for such a tragedy, but that too is understandable.

14   **The Civil War and Its Prisons**

It occurred only days after President Lincoln's assassination. The war had just ended; John Wilkes Booth, Lincoln's killer, had just been slain himself; and Jefferson Davis was sought as a possible Booth conspirator, which he was not; and as leader of the rebellion. The North's relief and joy over victory was tempered with shock and grief for the president and a desire for retribution. Thus, too many things were happening simultaneously, and the *Sultana* disappeared from the front pages of the North's newspapers in a surprisingly brief time for so great a disaster.

What was left of the *Sultana* disappeared as well beneath the mud of the ever-changing Mississippi. But a century and a quarter later the remains of the old steamboat may have been found covered by what now is Arkansas farmland. The old prison site on the bank of the Alabama also has been rediscovered. So Cahaba Federal Prison and the people involved are remembered again, if indeed they were ever truly forgotten.

2
The Town and
Its Prison

Cahaba seemed ready to flourish again with the coming of the 1860s. The Cahaba, Marion and Greensborough Rail Road was partially finished, running almost as an arrow from Marion, to the northwest and the county seat of the adjoining county. The gleaming new rails brought with them hope for a return to the former days when Cahaba bustled with commerce and importance. The tracks ran right down the middle of dusty, unpaved Capitol Street through the heart of town to the Alabama River. There train and steamboat exchanged cargo and passengers. Montgomery was up the river, the seaport of Mobile down, and the railroad-steamboat connection provided the most modern communications. Now a broad area, it was hoped, would send produce to the Cahaba rail terminus where the steamboats could start it to the world.

Cahaba sprawled along the west bank of the Alabama, being longer than wide, and the town's northern end snuggled against the smaller Cahaba River where it meets the Alabama. Oddly, the lesser of the two rivers is the one that most bedeviled Cahaba. There had been none of the terrible hope-killing floods for nearly thirty years, however, and the railroad promised to make the town a prime inland port again.

Joseph Babcock and John P. Fulks, founders of the Cahaba and Tuscaloosa Telegraph Company and owners of warehouses on the Alabama's bank on the north side of Capitol Street, were among those trusting in Cahaba's future. As an inducement to the railroad, they deeded to it for a dollar on February 23, 1860, land they owned along the river bank on the south side of the street. The railroad could have the land, Lots Four and Five, as long as it maintained its Cahaba depot. But Joseph Babcock died and Samuel M. Hill purchased for an undisclosed sum the other warehouses and land, plus the remaining Babcock and Fulks interest in the railroad's two lots, on June 21, 1861. The reason is apparent: more construction and progress. Hill also signed an eleven-year lease with the railroad for its interest in Lots Four and Five, agreeing to build a new warehouse costing at least $13,400 to substantially increase the storage capacity and business potential of the town for the goods that mattered most, cotton and corn.[1]

At Cahaba, however, prospects always brightened only briefly, and hope was but a passerby. Samuel Hill, a wealthy merchant and planter known as Colonel Hill, began constructing his warehouse of red bricks. The walls were up and all except the middle portion of the roof finished when circumstances forced a permanent halt. The railroad failed, never amounting to more than an unimportant and unprofitable little spur of twenty-five miles. Rails became precious when the war began, and the Cahaba, Marion and Greensborough never reached Greensborough. Now the Confederacy wanted the iron and other assets of the tiny railroad because it urgently needed ma-

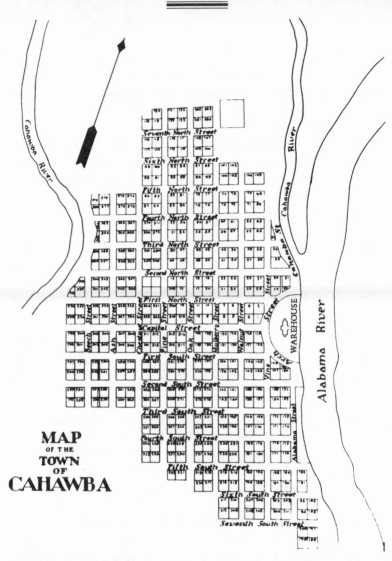

This is a map of Cahaba drawn in 1819 before the state began selling lots. It is the way planners intended Cahaba to look. Various changes were made in the actual construction, but the map shows how the Cahaba River curls around the town before emptying into the Alabama. Castle Morgan was a number of yards south of where the warehouse appears on the map.

18   The Town and Its Prison

terial to finish the strategically important Alabama and Mississippi Rivers Railroad from Selma to Demopolis to Meridian, an important segment of the only major trans-South rail artery in the lower Confederacy. That road crossed Cahaba's, which government agent A. S. Gaines said was "now doing nobody much good," fourteen miles west of Selma. The Confederate Congress showed the value attached to the bigger line by voting $150,000 to complete the last segments between Demopolis and Meridian, and the House requested by resolution that President Jefferson Davis inquire into the construction's progress. Gaines, a civil engineer from Demopolis appointed to push the work, reported to Secretary of War George W. Randolph on June 25, 1862, that he obtained from the Cahaba, Marion and Greensborough 55,367 pounds of spikes, 3,810 pounds of bolts and nuts, 17,636 pounds of iron fish bars used to strengthen rails, and 1,276 rails. For a time, a question of payment remained, but the Alabama and Mississippi Rivers Railroad largely was completed. The Tombigbee River at Demopolis remained unspanned, but by April 15, 1863, the A&MR daily ran two trains each way from Selma to Demopolis, a passenger train and a freight with a capacity of a hundred tons. On July 21 James A. Seddon, the new secretary of war, instructed D. H. Kenney of the Engineer Bureau in Richmond to see to the purchase or impressment of the remaining iron and rolling stock of the Cahaba, Marion and Greensborough.[2]

When the railroad died, it carried with it the original need for Colonel Hill's warehouse. The Confederacy, however, which had little and needed everything, soon found use even for a warehouse with an unfinished roof.

The few writers or historians who have mentioned Cahaba Federal Prison usually have placed it in one of Babcock's warehouses. Proof that the prison instead was in

Colonel Hill's building came in 1986 when an archaeologist found the dirt-covered remains of an old structure on Lots Four and Five. Her excavation uncovered walls of the right dimensions, evidence of the wooden stockade around the brick walls, remnants of the small reservoir made of barrels that stored the prison water, the ditch that carried water to the prison, traces of an interior room, and the place where the prisoners' water closet stood.[3] Everything corresponded to the information in the surviving prison records, proving she found the true site of the prison, something forgotten for decades.

The Confederacy appropriated Colonel Hill's warehouse around the middle of 1863. Historians previously have assumed from the available evidence that it was in October. However, a letter from Captain H. A. M. Henderson to Secretary of War Seddon, dated June 20, 1863, was found in Henderson's military records. Henderson, then at Demopolis, headquarters for the military Department of Alabama, Mississippi, and East Louisiana, requested permission to recruit men to be taken to Cahaba where they would be "employed as a guard for Federal prisoners so long as it may be necessary to maintain that post."[4] This shows the prison was opened as early as June, possibly sooner.

The thick brick walls of the warehouse stood fourteen feet high and measured 193 feet by 116 feet on the outside, enclosing 15,000 square feet. To make it a proper prison, officials ordered a stockade of two-inch planks, set 3 feet into the ground and standing 12 feet high, constructed around the warehouse. A plank walkway at the top gave guards an elevated position. Wooden bunks built one above the other under the roofed portions slept 432 men, but without straw or bedding, none ever being provided. The water closet, at the southeast corner, accommodated 4 men at once. Water came from a gushing natural spring,

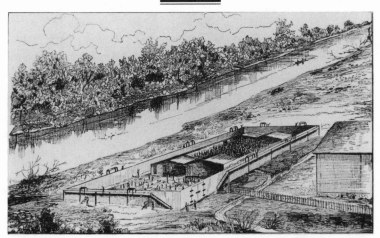

Castle Morgan as Jesse Hawes remembered it. Note the guards' walk-way at the top of the stockade wall and the ditch carrying water into the prison. The building at right would be the home of Mrs. Amanda Gardner. (Jesse Hawes, *Cahaba: A Story of Captive Boys in Blue*)

one of more than seventy in the town, which emptied into an open street gutter and flowed uncovered for two hundred yards before running under the stockade and across the prison through a ditch, exiting through the water closet.[5]

Apparently Henderson's guard force was insufficient, for on March 29, 1864, the Selma *Morning Reporter* printed orders for unassigned men to report for duty at Cahaba, where "all the Federal prisoners captured in the Depart-ment are confined." The newspaper repeated the call in later issues. On April 11, the newspaper included orders dated March 25 from Demopolis instructing post com-manders to send captured Federal soldiers to Cahaba, where Lieutenant Colonel Henry C. Davis "is ordered by the War Department to receive and hold all such pris-

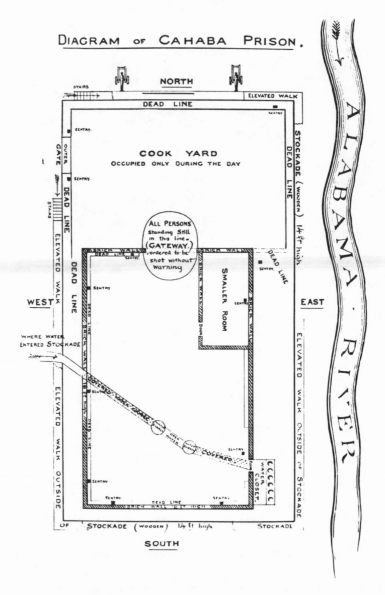

Jesse Hawes's diagram of the prison (Jesse Hawes, *Cahaba: A Story of Captive Boys in Blue*)

22 The Town and Its Prison

oners." Captain H. A. M. Henderson was listed as Davis's adjutant.[6]

Despite this evidence that the prison was just being put into full use, R. H. Whitfield, the prison surgeon, said in a report dated March 31, 1864, that the place had been open for five months and held 660 men. His report is the earliest mention of the prison in the official war records, and provides a vivid description.[7]

Conditions distressed Whitfield, who also had served at Vicksburg. He complained that intolerable pollution invaded the water on its long course from well to prison, including the "washings of the hands, feet, faces, and heads of soldiers, citizens, and negroes, buckets, tubs, and spittoons of groceries, offices and hospital, hogs, dogs, cows, and horses, and filth of all kinds from the streets and other sources."[8]

Whitfield said the covered parts of the warehouse had four open windows and an earthen floor, and the unfinished portion of the roof left 1,600 (square) feet of open space in the center. The building included only one fireplace and men cooked on as many as forty open fires, using green pine or decayed oak gathered from fields, and creating an intolerable amount of smoke. The men had only a single wheelbarrow to remove filth and rubbish from the entire prison, resulting in "an unavoidable accumulation of these fruitful sources of disease." He complained also that the quartermasters "with only this prison and one small hospital to supply," failed to provide suitable wood, water, and bunks, and to keep the prison "in a condition to which it would be moderately comfortable, clean and healthy."

The surgeon sent his report a little more than a month after Andersonville received its first prisoners on February 17, and Samuel Cooper, adjutant and inspector general of Confederate armies, ordered on April 24 that Cahaba be

The Town and Its Prison 23

closed and the men and their guards transferred to Andersonville. Lieutenant Colonel Davis confirmed compliance on May 3. He said no prisoners remained except those too sick to travel.[9]

Cahaba Federal Prison, however, was not closed. The *Morning Reporter* printed an item on May 13 that said Cahaba remained a receiving depot for the department, and that as soon as five hundred prisoners "accumulate, they will be sent forward to the great central depot in Georgia." The newspaper said about fifteen hundred Federal soldiers already had been transferred.[10]

In two months the Confederacy again turned to Cahaba as a full-time prison. Heavy and almost constant fighting and the halt in exchanges following Lieutenant General Grant's rise to the Union military summit resulted in the South's taking, and having to keep, large numbers of prisoners. They swamped Andersonville, and Cahaba soon became swamped as well, with more than two thousand men crowded together in the stockaded warehouse on the Alabama.[11]

Although Cahaba Federal Prison was the official name, the prison was known locally as Castle Morgan in honor of the famed Confederate cavalry general John Hunt Morgan. How it came to be so called is uncertain. None of the prisoners apparently knew and this name does not appear in the official records. However, Morgan made his famous escape from the Ohio State Penitentiary at Columbus on the night of November 27, 1863, a few months after the opening of Cahaba prison.[12]

Establishment of such an unhappy place seems an unfitting last chapter for a town started with grand plans by men who dreamed of making it a great city. However, Cahaba, which did not simply evolve at a convenient location as do so many cities, but was carved deliberately from a wilderness, never had much of a chance despite the hopes of its founders and the wishes of its champions, and did not last very long after 1865. Melvin Grigsby, a prisoner who returned nearly twenty years after the war, found a town virtually deserted and the warehouse and stockade gone. A lush growth of weeds covered the prison ground. In a book published in 1888, he quoted an old black man who operated a ferry over the Cahaba River as telling him the city simply had been moved to Selma, which was exactly what happened to Cahaba. Colonel Hill, apparently financially ruined by the war, lost his warehouse in a sheriff's sale recorded on May 10, 1869. It brought $195. The last mention of the building in Dallas County records was another sale, this time for $285.21, on May 24, 1871.[13] The former prison apparently was dismantled and the bricks carried to Selma.

Both the town and the river originally were called *Cahawba*, likely a corruption of the Choctaw *Oka Uba*, the Indian name for the river. It means "water above," which stems either from the Indians knowing well the river's propensity to flood, or the river's flowing from the north. The Alabama, in contrast, meanders from the east before turning its sensuous course south at Selma. The narrow but beautiful, clear, and swift Cahaba begins northeast of Birmingham, which did not exist during Cahaba's days, and makes a giant loop to the west before keeping its rendezvous at Cahaba with the much larger Alabama. Four hundred years ago an Indian village called *Casiste* occupied the same ground at the river junction. The French had a trading post called *Caba* there two hundred years later. They abandoned it around 1740 because of Indian attacks.[14]

No discernible pattern exists in the use of *Cahawba* and *Cahaba*. Writers and historians employ both. Major Howell Tatum, in his "Topographical Notes and Observations on the Alabama River, August, 1814," spelled it *Cau-hau-ba*.[15]

Both the census records of the decades before the Civil War and most of the official records of the war used *Cahaba*, but *Cahawba* apparently was the original name of river and town.

A few years after General Andrew Jackson defeated the Indians and deprived them of their lands during the War of 1812, the territorial government, which sat in Saint Stephens, sought a more central location for a permanent capital, since the territory was becoming a state. A commission picked the land at the mouth of the Cahaba, and the government began to have a town carved from the woods on ground thought sufficiently high to make the area immune from flooding. Statesmen saw the two rivers as important highways of commerce destined to make the capital at their junction a metropolis.

Governor William Wyatt Bibb told the Territorial Assembly on November 8, 1818: "The bluff on the west side of those rivers presents a beautiful scite [*sic*], with springs of good water and the prospects of health. Situated on a river capable of being navigated by boates [*sic*] of great burthen, and supported as it will be by the abundant production of an extensive and fertile back country on the Alabama and Cahawba and their tributary streams the town of Cahawba promises to vie with the largest inland towns in the country."[16]

The Cahaba's course marks off a large horseshoe just before the river joins the Alabama, going well south on the western side of the town and then looping back north before turning south again to empty into the Alabama. The prongs of the open end of the horseshoe straddle the northern portion of the town. The Alabama forms the eastern border and tiny Clear Creek the western, making the area a peninsula untouched by water only on the south. Into this peninsula the territorial government moved. Cahaba was incorporated and became the capital in 1819. It also was the county seat of Dallas County and growth was rapid. Hundreds rushed to embrace the rich prospects offered by a new capital city in the wilderness. Let the Craigs, who became a leading family, serve as one example.[17]

They were from Antrim County in Ireland, leaving there for South Carolina shortly after the American War for Independence. Several Craigs responded to the lure of the wild interior, some going to Tennessee where they found the terrain rugged and farming unrewarding except on low land along the rivers. Thomas Craig took his wife and children to Alabama, stopping for a season to grow corn at a sparsely inhabited place which would become Montgomery. With his harvest as capital, he moved west and opened a ferry over the Cahaba River in 1817. He also farmed, and he sent word to Tennessee for other Craigs to join him after Cahaba became a bustling new place. His nephew, James D. Craig, told in his unpublished memoirs of rafting cedar logs cut at Cahaba down the winding Alabama to Mobile Bay to be loaded onto British ships. They were used in England to moth-proof buildings where wool was stored. For this he was paid fifty cents a day and deck passage back up the river on the steamboat *Columbus*. The boy who rafted logs grew to become a lawyer, Dallas County clerk, the father of nine, and a plantation owner with ninety slaves.[18] By 1861 he had gathered a fortune of about half a million dollars, all lost during the war. He said in his memoirs:

We enjoyed up to the war the best of society, churches, schools and sociable intercourse, and not excelled in any community of its size. But the cruel war waged against us by our Northern Brethern [*sic*] on account of the fact that we owned slaves, and ended in the total abolition of slavery, and the detoriation [*sic*] of all our property. So that at the end thereof, we were ruined. Totally ruined, all our negroes set free, and everybody in debt and no money to pay with. We had to commence a new system of labor which will be in the end better for all.

He abandoned Cahaba for Selma in 1869 and then followed other family members to California. He became commissioner of the San Francisco Superior Court, a position he held at his death in 1882 at the age of eighty-one.

For a time Cahaba flourished in the wilderness. It was the capital when Lafayette made a triumphal return to the United States in 1825. The French hero of the American Revolution spent three days there. Alabama entertained him with parades, banquets, and visits by members of Napoleon's old Imperial Guard who founded Demopolis, about forty miles to the west. River craft served as Governor Bibb expected, and the town had two newspapers, a land office, a state bank, schools, shops, hotels, and plantations all around.[19]

Disaster, however, was not long delayed. Governor Bibb and his fellow creators of Cahaba foresaw much in the capital's potential but nothing in the destructive potential of the rivers. They did not know that when the rivers filled with heavy rains, the Cahaba had no place to go when it reached the Alabama, the massive current of the bigger river acting as a dam. The Cahaba then went over its banks and ravaged the land. The first great flood occurred in 1825, the year of Lafayette's visit. Fortunately, he was gone before the water wrecked the town, becoming so high that Alabama's legislators entered the statehouse by boat.[20]

The Senate's Seat of Government Committee recommended that same year that the government find another capital. It reported that part of Cahaba flooded often and reaching the town became impossible even on horseback. The government moved to Tuscaloosa in 1826, before permanent settlement in Montgomery, and Cahaba for a time dwindled. Another flood came in 1833, but the town remained the seat of Dallas County and still important, and its remaining people persisted until it flourished again. As farms and plantations in Dallas and surrounding counties grew in numbers and abundance, it became one of the most important shipping points on the Alabama River. It reached its peak growth by 1850, its population approaching 5,000, including slaves. But by then it lay under the shadow of nearby Selma, which was situated on a bluff a hundred feet above the Alabama and completely protected from flooding. By 1860 Cahaba's population had dwindled to 680 whites and about 2,000 slaves. The war and the flood of 1865 killed all prospects for the town, and Selma became the county seat the next year, the year after the war ended. In 1870 the Cahaba population was but 431, most of the inhabitants former slaves.[21]

Cahaba, which stretched north-south along the Alabama for several hundred yards, was only ten to twenty feet above the rivers. Capitol Street ran east-west through the middle of the town. Near the Alabama it was crossed by Arch Street, a sunken road that archaeologists believe may have been a defensive moat for the Indians in the distant past. Arch Street was so named because of its shape, being a semicircle with both ends on the Alabama.[22] If one turns a map of the town so that the west is at the top, the street looks as though it forms an arch. Inside the half-circle made by the street was an open area, and in that area sat the warehouses of Joseph Babcock and John P. Fulks, and the unfinished warehouse of Colonel Samuel Hill.

By June 1864 conditions at Andersonville were desperate. So many hungry Federal soldiers swarmed Camp Sumter, the official name of that prison, that Richmond became alarmed. General William T. Sherman's armies were just outside Marietta, Georgia, not far from Atlanta, and steadily forcing the smaller Confederate army of General Joseph E. Johnston back toward the important railroad and supply center. Fearing Sherman might send a cavalry raid to Andersonville, Richmond ordered Brigadier General John H. Winder to select a location in Alabama—either Cahaba or Union Springs—to which a portion of Andersonville's inmates could be transferred, since "it is not desirable to keep a large body of prisoners together." Winder, who was in command of all prisons in Alabama and Georgia, instructed Captain C. E. Dyke of the Florida Light Artillery to inspect the two places suggested.

Unaccountably Captain Dyke misinterpreted his orders to mean that he was to visit Cahaba only if he found Union Springs unsuitable. He did not go to Cahaba and did not like what he found at Union Springs, reporting that the town had limited water despite its name. But he chanced upon Silver Run, a community in Russell County on the Alabama-Georgia border about twenty miles south of Columbus. Silver Run, now the town of Seale, was "admirably adapted to the purpose required," Dyke said in his report to Captain W. Sidney Winder, the general's adjutant and son. "Timber, water, everything requisite is at hand, directly on the railroad."[23]

General Winder telegraphed Richmond on July 7: "After examinations, Silver Run, twenty miles from Columbus, Ga., on the road to Union Springs, Ala., is the most suitable place to establish a depot for prisoners of war. Neither Cahaba nor Union Springs will answer. Silver Run every way suitable. Shall I proceed to establish the depot?"[24]

The following day, President W. H. Mitchell of the little Mobile and Girard (Phenix City) Railroad, which passed through Silver Run but had not been built beyond Union Springs, fewer than fifty miles away, wrote Secretary of War Seddon that he understood "a spot on this road" might become a prison site. He suggested such a facility would consume part of the region's supplies and "be an injury to the army stores of provisions." He said, "There are countless thousands of bushels of grain west of the Alabama River that can not be made available for the want of transportation," and suggested a location west of Selma. "It is a better provision country and equally as safe and healthy."[25]

General Winder, nevertheless, pressed for construction of a prison at Silver Run, telegraphing Adjutant General Cooper on July 13, "Please get authority for me to impress labor and teams to establish the prison at Silver Run, Ala." Three days later he wired Cooper again: "Silver Run is the most convenient place that I can hear of."[26]

Meanwhile, Sherman's armies pressed closer to Atlanta. On July 11 General Johnston, then defending the crossings of the Chattahoochee River within sight of the city, sent a message to General Braxton Bragg in Richmond strongly recommending immediate redistribution of the prisoners at Andersonville. Bragg, President Davis' close friend and military adviser, was in Atlanta four days later to study the military crisis, and from there sent a terse telegraph to Adjutant General Cooper that settled the matter: "No more prisoners should be sent this side of South Carolina for the present. Have ordered the new depot at Cahaba and the transfer immediately."[27]

Alabama Governor Thomas H. Watts received an explanation for the rejection of Silver Run from President Davis on August 25. The president wired him: "Conditions to be fulfilled in selection of a prison depot are nearness to subsistence, not now available for Armies of Tennessee and Virginia, and safety from raids. Silver Run is in a region drained for both armies, and liable to raids in Sherman's present position."[28]

Thus Colonel Hill's warehouse again became a full-time prison. But no large-scale transfer of prisoners from Andersonville to Cahaba occurred. They went instead to Charleston, Savannah, Florence, and later a new prison at

Millen, Georgia. Cahaba, however, had no want for inmates. Within three months their numbers climbed toward three thousand.[29] It will be recalled that surgeon Whitfield thought conditions poor when only 660 men lived on that sandy third of an acre.

A few improvements were made. More of the rough plank bunks were added, but never more than 600, and there was no bedding of any sort. Guards locked the men in the warehouse at night and all without bunks found restless sleep on bare ground. The water no longer ran through an open ditch, but came from the clear spring to the prison through pipes. Three sunken barrels, their rims at ground level, served as reservoirs, but the water was high in sulfur and the men found it distasteful.[30]

Colonel D. T. Chandler, an army inspector general, arrived in October to survey conditions, and found little he approved. He filed a lengthy report on October 16.[31]

Chandler said the prison was intended for 500, but then held 2,151, of whom 69 were hospitalized and another 75 needed to be. The hospital, however, had insufficient space. Open fires were the only means of warming the warehouse and produced choking smoke inside the enclosure. The men received a "very insufficient" supply of cooking utensils and only three worn-out axes to chop up the logs provided as fuel. The quartermaster issued food raw and it consisted exclusively of bread and meat, only two issues of rice having been made although the guards received it daily. The prisoners received no peas or beans, "those on hand being utterly unfit for use." No vinegar, then thought to be an excellent general purpose medicine and specific for intestinal disorder, fever and aches, had been issued although "good vinegar could readily be obtained at Mobile by writing for it. . . . Great suffering and much sickness will necessarily occur among the prisoners during this winter from the impracticability of making fires inside the building and the inability to furnish them with proper clothing and bedding."

The guard, Chandler said, included the Trans-Mississippi Battalion, 55 men; two companies of Alabama infantry reserves, 82 men; one company of Alabama reserve cavalry, 24 men; and 18 men assigned various details, making a total of 179. About 50 of the men were under orders from Richmond to report to the Army of Tennessee but could not be released until replaced. Arms included two small pieces of field artillery. The guards, Chandler said, were inferior in both discipline and instruction. "Owing to the small number, they are on duty every other day, and they are totally inadequate for the duties required of them."

Chandler then added a warning of what might be the consequences of keeping so many prisoners in crowded and unhappy conditions under an inadequate guard. He said they were divided into companies of 100 and squads of 10 for police and messing purposes, giving them the rudiments of organization. They, he said, "need only a little determination and a leader to enable them at any time to overpower the feeble garrison. Some few might be killed, but the majority could easily effect their escape." Should a mass escape occur, Chandler warned, the district was defenseless except for scattered details and a small provost guard at Selma. The entire area would be at the mercy of a large group of hungry, angry, desperate Union soldiers.

Having detailed the problems and the possibilities, Chandler recommended that the prison be moved a mile to the south where the plantation of Joel E. Mathews included ground suitable for a stockade of from ten to twenty-five acres.[32] The high and level site had good water, timber, and a sawmill, and "its distance from the river renders it more healthy and safe." Logs for the prisoners' fires came from the plantation, he said, the wood prisoners once foraged from nearby fields having been consumed.

The inspector general filed a diagram of the prison showing improvements he suggested if it remained at the old site.[33] These included widening the area enclosed by the stockade and extending it by thirty-five feet on the north, providing more room for daytime use. Included also was an increase in the size of the water closet and the addition of a small cook house and bakery against the north wall of the expanded stockade. Previously it was not known whether the changes shown in the diagram were made, there being no later mention in the official records. But archaeological evidence demonstrates that the recommended additions were constructed. The extension on the north, indeed, carried the stockade right into the middle of Capitol Street, right up to where the railroad tracks had been.[34]

Colonel Chandler's report made its way through the Confederate chain of command to Secretary of War Seddon, who sent it to L. B. Northrop, commissary general of the southern army, "for special and prompt attention."[35] This resulted in a sharp reply on November 5 from Northrop, the man charged with supplying all the needs of the Confederate armies and their captives as well. The reply illustrates the difficulties of the South and the necessary priorities:

Respectfully returned to the Secretary of War.

It is not considered necessary to refer this paper for explanation, for the Commissary-General is aware that the facts are in general as stated. The means of obtaining supplies afforded this Bureau in officers, men, and money are entirely insufficient to enable it to provide for the large number of troops in the field more than the actual necessaries of life, and it cannot be expected that the prisoners shall fare better than our own men. If from

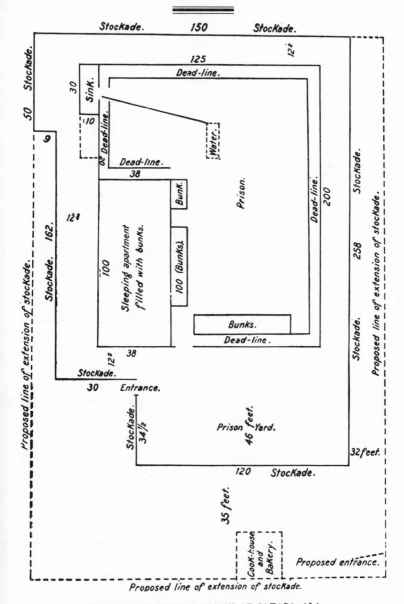

DIAGRAM OF FEDERAL PRISON AT CAHABA, ALA.

The diagram Colonel Chandler sent with his inspection report on Cahaba Federal Prison. It includes suggested improvements, which excavation at the site indicates were made. (*The War of the Rebellion: A Compilation of the Official Records of the Union and Confederate Armies*) the circumstances it is possible to give these less necessary articles to only a small number of a post the prisoners shall not be the first to enjoy them.[36]

In sum, General Northrop felt too many obstacles and inadequate means hindered his major work, supplying the southern armies. He did not think he should be bothered about the plight of a few captives in Alabama, since he could do little for them. In no event would they be better supplied than southern soldiers. If anything extra were available, it would not go to prisoners of war. He would not worry about vinegar for the aches, fevers, and intestinal disorders of Union men if southern men in the armies needed it.

Three days after Chandler filed his report, and before General Northrop drafted his pointed reply, Adjutant General Cooper made a small effort to help. He wired General Winder: "The surplus prisoners at Cahaba should be transferred to Millen." This was not done, although about four hundred went to Meridian instead by order of Lieutenant General Richard Taylor, commander of the department, some of them being returned later. In addition, more than a hundred sick and wounded left on November 21 for Savannah in a special exchange of prisoners.[37] The prison was not moved. Other than the new construction, Colonel Chandler's report drew no response after General Northrop's impatient dismissal. The men inside the warehouse and stockade on the bank of the Alabama would have to wait for relief. Some did not last long enough, and for many more their release from prison would be but a prelude to something worse and much more deadly.

3
The Commanders

Men of dramatic contrast shared authority over the inmates of Cahaba Federal Prison, one considerate and likable, the other choleric and detested. Captain Henderson, a Methodist minister, was much admired by the prisoners and also admired by some of the Federal officers he met under flag of truce. They became friends, and by his own account, which there is no reason to doubt, the Federal army provided him a bodyguard of cavalry during a dangerous time on the Mississippi near the end of the war. He used his good relations with Union men to arrange a steamboat load of clothing, blankets, medicines, and other Federal supplies for the Cahaba prisoners, and he played a part in the early release of thousands of captured soldiers from both sides.[1]

After the war, Henderson became a newspaper editor briefly at Demopolis before returning to Kentucky and the ministry. He served two terms as state superintendent of education in Kentucky and later became pastor of the Jersey City church attended by the sister and mother of President Grant. When Hannah Simpson Grant died in 1883,

Henderson presided at her funeral, the former commander of a Confederate prison camp saying the last words over the mortal remains of the mother of the Union's foremost soldier. It is not known whether the Grant family knew of his wartime service. He also served, at age sixty-two, in the Spanish-American War.[2]

Lieutenant Colonel Jones, on the other hand, apparently was a bitter man who scoffed at the discomfort of the prisoners and was accused of murdering one. He succeeded Lieutenant Colonel Davis as head of the military post at Cahaba, which included the small guard force, whereas Henderson became commander of the prison and its inmates. Since Henderson also served as a Confederate agent for the exchange of prisoners, appointed on August 14, 1863, he often visited behind Union lines, usually at Memphis or Vicksburg, to negotiate or to escort men scheduled for special exchange. In his absence, the draconian Jones held all power at both post and prison.[3]

Jones was from New Orleans. According to Jesse Hawes, he worked as a bookkeeper in a large wholesale house. Jones began the war as a member of the Allen Guards, joining on August 19, 1861, four months after Fort Sumter. Despite the prisoners' harsh opinion, he apparently was a good and dedicated soldier. He became a captain commanding his own company and arrived at Fort Jackson, on the Mississippi River below New Orleans, on November 8, 1861. During a reorganization, the Guards were assigned to the Twenty-third Louisiana Volunteers, with Jones's men becoming Company I. Although officially listed as infantry, several of the Twenty-third's units previously made up the Orleans Battalion, Louisiana Artillery, and the regiment manned the heavy guns of Fort Jackson. It participated in the defense of that fort and Fort Saint Philip across the river during the Union campaign that resulted in the capture of New Orleans. The forts fell on

April 28, 1862, after a crushing bombardment by the U.S. Navy. About half the defenders mutinied and fled, which heavily contributed to the Confederate disaster. Jones was captured with those who stayed by the guns to the end, and soon was paroled. There was no question of his soldierly qualities, and Lieutenant Colonel Edward Higgins, commander of the two forts, named him in the official after-action report as among the officers who "fought their batteries gallantly and well."[4]

The regiment was exchanged, meaning the men were free to rejoin southern ranks, but it nearly dissolved when many of the remaining troops refused further service, saying they enlisted for Louisiana and would not campaign outside the fallen Confederate state.

Jones, however, remained true to his cause and led men still willing to fight to Vicksburg. There the regiment received a new name, the Twenty-second Louisiana, and Jones won promotion to lieutenant colonel commanding the unit on May 2, 1863.[5] During Grant's siege of Vicksburg, Jones's artillerymen served with the river batteries led by his former commander at Fort Jackson, Colonel Higgins. All were captured on the city's surrender, July 4, 1863, and for the second time in little more than a year, Jones became a prisoner of war and was paroled. Despite a date of rank preceding his second capture by two months and the prior change in the regiment's designation, Jones for some reason signed his Vicksburg parole, dated July 8, as captain, not lieutenant colonel, commanding the Twenty-third, not the Twenty-second.[6]

Jones could not know it, but his days of leading combat soldiers ended with the fall of Vicksburg. The Twenty-second was consolidated at Enterprise, Mississippi, in January 1864, with other understrength units. While the new regiment retained the Twenty-second's name, it being the largest of the eight units involved, Jones was passed over for command in favor of Colonel Isaac W. Patton, who outranked Jones and came to the merger with the Twenty-first Louisiana. An unhappy Jones then became chief provost marshal for the third district of Alabama, with headquarters in Montgomery.

One of the reasons Jones lost command may have involved a mistake he made while still a green officer early in the war. He changed an endorsement by General David E. Twiggs on a muster roll by inserting the word *Confederate*. The surviving records are incomplete and unclear, but apparently Jones intended to differentiate between Confederate and state forces. As insignificant as the matter may have seemed to Jones, he had impertinently altered on his own the already-approved document of a high-ranking superior officer, and the Confederacy finally got around to a court-martial. Jones explained in a letter to Lieutenant Colonel Thomas M. Jack, on the staff of General Leonidas Polk, then commanding the department: "The word was added by me in order to carry out the sense and meaning of Gen. Twiggs when he ordered the endorsement made on the muster-roll. I never made any concealment of my having done so, but on the contrary openly stated the fact."[7]

The military court, sitting at Enterprise, Mississippi, early in 1864, found the action "to have been very improper," but acquitted Jones and ordered him returned to duty.[8] Jones, by then already handling his military police functions at Montgomery, wrote several letters to his superiors, before and after the decision, pleading for promotion to full colonel and reinstatement as commander of the Twenty-second Louisiana, then at Mobile. He said Colonel Patton was absent without leave, probably unable to return after a trip home to Union-held New Orleans, leaving the regiment without proper command. Saying also that Patton had no experience with heavy artillery, he offered to stand an examination on his own skill with big guns. He included a quotation from a letter he said he received from another officer of the Twenty-second, whom he did not identify.

We had the gratification of hearing read on dress parade several evenings since the proceedings and findings of the Military Court in your case, and it was a pleasure to all to hear that you had triumphed over your enemies and came out of the fire of their malice unscathed. I am unable to give you any positive information of Col. Patton beyond that he is in New Orleans without leave since 29th February, although not so reported. It seems strange that he should remain so long. . . . A rumor was current a day or so ago that he had gone to West Louisiana to report to [Confederate General] Kirby Smith. I give it for what it is worth. . . . Many of us and especially myself would hail your return with delight . . . our regiment (consolidated I mean) is actually going to the——[blank in the original] for want of proper attention on the part of the officers. Hence, I wish the return of one who would endeavor to make a reformation in the discipline of the regiment.[9]

Clumsy preening for his superiors with the accolades of an unidentified friend did Jones no good, however. He pleaded uselessly. He would not again see his beloved Louisiana unit. He instead was assigned to the post of Cahaba by Major General Dabney H. Maury, commanding the District of the Gulf, on July 28, 1864. Colonel Patton, meanwhile, returned from New Orleans to command Jones's regiment and its guns at Spanish Fort in upper Mobile Bay, taking part in the futile defense of Mobile in March and April 1865.[10]

Jones's loss of his regiment and the injury to his reputation and ego may help explain the bitterness, evidenced by consistent ill temper, even murderous ill temper, carried to Cahaba Federal Prison by a man who twice was a prisoner of war himself.

Apparently Jones's appointment to Cahaba was a surprise outside the district and certainly among those who ran the Confederacy's prison system. It was questioned by Brigadier General Winder, who wrote Adjutant and Inspector General Cooper on October 27, 1864, listing the post commanders at his prisons. He included last the name of Lieutenant Colonel Jones at Cahaba. "How this latter officer got into command I am not informed, the only information being a letter in which he signs himself as commander of the post. I think I should be informed when a change is made in the prisons under my control."[11]

Cooper's office looked into the records in Richmond but could find nothing on Jones's assignment, and he remained at Cahaba until the prisoners were released during the final weeks of the war, then taking command of the post at Demopolis.[12]

Cooper did not favor divided authority such as at Cahaba, as shown by his handling of Colonel Chandler's inspection of the prison, filed only days before Winder complained about Jones. Cooper had his assistant, R. H. Chilton, forward the report to the secretary of war with the notation: "This prison is another exemplification of the necessity of placing all under the control of one competent officer."[13] The suggestion bred no action, however, and Cahaba continued to have one commander too many. Almost nothing is known of Jones's prewar life, and history's last word from him was his third and final parole, signed at Meridian, Mississippi, on May 17, 1865, at the war's end.[14]

Much more may be discovered about Henderson. His full name was Howard Andrew Millett Henderson. He was born in August 1836 at Paris, Kentucky, in Bourbon County. His father, Howard H. Henderson, was a New

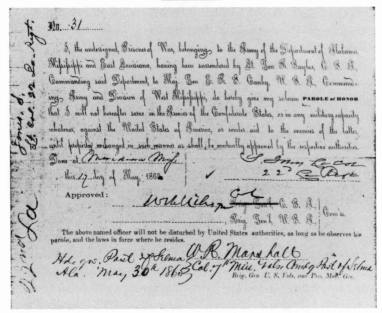

History's last word from Lieutenant Colonel Sam Jones. This is his last parole at the end of the war, signed at Meridian, Mississippi. (National Archives)

Hampshire native and graduate of Exeter Academy and Yale College. He moved to Paris to become president of a college for women and married one of his students, Jane Elizabeth Moore. Their son, who grew to stand only five feet, six inches, and had brown eyes and dark hair, graduated from Ohio Wesleyan University at Delaware, Ohio. He studied also at the Cincinnati Law School. He was ordained in the Methodist ministry and assigned to Demopolis. There he married Susan Watkins Vaughan, daughter of a physician and planter, and became the father of a daughter, Ada. A Demopolis resident wrote of Henderson: "This young pulpit orator, pastor of the Episcopal Metho-

The Commanders 43

dist Church, South, of Demopolis . . . became thoroughly incorporated in the community in every sense. He was possessed of remarkable oratorical power. His voice was clear and resonant and his manner graceful."[15]

Henderson believed ardently in states' rights and led the oratory at Demopolis in favor of Alabama abandoning the Union. He marched at the head of a torchlight parade celebrating approval of the state's Ordinance of Secession, and entered Confederate military service on February 18, 1862, ten months after Fort Sumter, as organizer and commander of Company E, Twenty-eighth Alabama Infantry. He resigned the following September, saying he was "unable to discharge the duties of an officer of an army in the field on account of an enfeebled constitution and a progressive disease." Apparently he recovered at home, for he soon was acting provost marshal for the post of Demopolis and, on June 20, 1863, wrote Secretary of War Seddon requesting appointment as captain and asking permission to raise a force of guards to serve at Cahaba.[16] His request was granted and he also was made assistant agent for exchange of prisoners.

Jesse Hawes of the Ninth Illinois Cavalry, wrote much about both Lieutenant Colonel Jones and Captain Henderson. Regarding Jones he asked: "By what strange and malignant destiny, if there was no method in it, were cowards and cruel men so often placed in charge of the prisons for Federal captives?" He quoted Jones as saying to a prisoner, "You damned Yankees will get enough of this kind of existence before you get out. If I could have my own way I would hang every devil of you." Jones once told a man detailed to bury a comrade, "I'm only sorry the damned blue-bellies are so tough—they don't die fast enough."[17]

Sergeant Hosea C. Aldrich of the Eighteenth Michigan Volunteer Infantry, quoted Jones as telling the captives when the prison was inundated by the rivers that they would remain in the flooded stockade until carried out to be buried. Hawes recalled a similar incident. He said Jones visited the stockade in a boat and replied to the prisoners' pleas to be allowed to leave the water and move to higher ground, "Not so long as there is a God-damned Yankee's head above water can you come out of that stockade."[18]

John L. Walker of the Fiftieth Ohio Volunteer Infantry, a native of Scotland who enlisted at Mount Jefferson, Ohio, also remembered Lieutenant Colonel Jones. During another period of heavy rain, the men were slow to prepare their beds in the mud under the wide unroofed portion of the warehouse. He said Jones told them, "If you don't find a place pretty soon, I'll find a grave for you before morning." Said Walker, "This same Colonel Samuel Jones was guilty of many, many inhuman acts to his unfortunate fellow beings. . . . Words fail me as I attempt to tell of his brutal conduct during those days of confinement in Castle Morgan. . . . He would frequently walk along the dead line, and finding a poor comrade sitting so close to it that an inch or two of his body happened to extend over, the only notice he would give this unfortunate fellow was a kick from his boot—not a word did he speak."[19]

Sergeant Emmet C. West remembered Jones while serving under George Armstrong Custer in Texas shortly after the war. He wrote bitterly of Custer's having soldiers whipped and otherwise abused. "I can compare his inhuman treatment of the men under him that summer to nothing I saw or experienced in my four years' service, but the inhuman treatment of the Union prisoners at Cahaba by Col. Jones."[20]

The men held different memories of Captain Henderson. Hawes related several incidents showing Henderson's concern for captives, such as his purchase of shoes for a barefoot young officer he escorted to Memphis for exchange, and his weeping at the death of another young Union soldier. The officer who received the shoes, identified by Hawes only as Captain Poe, reciprocated when freed at Memphis—and apparently paid—by taking Henderson to a clothing store and inducing him to accept a fine military overcoat as a gift of appreciation. Another soldier, a carriage-maker in civilian life who was paroled to remain outside the prison, made a miniature carriage for Henderson's little daughter, Ada, "who was much petted by our men outside." Hawes said the soldier became seriously ill with chronic diarrhea and dysentery, and Henderson arranged his exchange. He escorted the man to Vicksburg, the two riding on the train to Jackson and from there in an ambulance. Within sight of the U.S. flag flying from the Union camp, so close to freedom, the young soldier told Henderson, "Raise me up, please, I want to see our beautiful flag." When he saw the banner, he said, "Thank God! I shall see my dear wife and babies again." A few minutes later he "grew ashy pale, and sank lifeless into the arms of the Confederate, down whose cheeks the tears of sorrow and sympathy flowed."[21] Hawes did not explain how he became intimately acquainted from Castle Morgan with events in Memphis or Vicksburg, and the stories may be apocryphal. That he related them in detail, however, is a statement of his admiration.

He wrote, "It was often in the power of Henderson to extend kindnesses and courtesies to prisoners, and we are glad to note that the opportunity was not infrequently embraced." He began his pages on Henderson and Jones with: "In these memoirs of Cahaba a prominent place should be given to Captain (later Colonel) Howard A. M. Henderson." He said Henderson was "remembered with kindly wishes" by "many of the non-commissioned officers and privates."[22]

Walker wrote of Henderson: "He was a man who was

Castle Morgan's commander. H. A. M. Henderson served two terms as Kentucky's state school superintendent after the war. This photograph was taken during his service there. (*History of Education in Kentucky*)

held in the highest esteem by all the prisoners for his kind and considerate manner toward them at all times. This same Colonel Henderson has since become a Methodist minister and a resident of the North and is loved and respected by all who have ever met him."[23]

Henderson, of course, already was a Methodist minister, and while he wore the two hats of prison commander and assistant commissioner for the exchange of prisoners, he still found time to conduct frequent Sunday services at Cahaba's Methodist church.[24]

None of the prisoners left a description of Jones's physical appearance, and no photograph is known to exist. He apparently was energetic and efficient, if cruel and quick to anger. He was indifferent to the suffering of his helpless enemies, and probably guilty of murder. There is no evidence to support Hawes's contention of alcoholism and that Jones was "never seen by us except when intoxicated."[25] Jones's letters and messages show him as well educated and ambitious, determined, dedicated to his cause and duties. Although he did not so distinguish himself at Vicksburg, indications are he fought his artillery well when given a chance to command, and he merited mention in official reports. He put down the uprising in Castle Morgan quickly and efficiently, without loss of a prisoner or a serious casualty to either side. He pursued and recaptured most, if not all, who escaped the prison. To his credit, he stayed by his final post at Demopolis to the last hour as Confederate hope and pitiful resistance collapsed all about him. He relayed messages, forwarded orders, sought instructions. He clearly tried to maintain to the end an island of calm. He was among the last to quit.

Photographs of Henderson show a confident man with a broad forehead, strong chin, straight shoulders. He is clean-shaven except for a moderately thick moustache, its ends descending past the slightly down-turned corners of his mouth. The lips are thin and pressed together as if in determination. He was humane to his enemies as demonstrated by all reports. He was a gentle man who maintained just enough aura of toughness in his official correspondence to satisfy his superiors. He too was energetic and handled his duties efficiently under the incurable handicap of limited resources always shrinking. He receives much of the credit for the low death toll at Castle Morgan among prisoners who, according to one, probably fared "better than the inmates of any other prison inside of the Confederate lines."[26]

4
The Men

The first arrivals at Castle Morgan, those who were inmates before the early transfer to Andersonville and before the coming of Lieutenant Colonel Jones, found conditions to be as disagreeable as might be expected, but not harsh. One of them, Melvin Grigsby of the Seventh Wisconsin Infantry, chiefly disliked sleeping on the ground without bedding or blankets. "Otherwise we had nothing to complain of," he said. "Our food was wholesome and sufficient."[1]

He said the two officers of the prison, a captain and a lieutenant whose names he could not remember, "were gentlemen. We did not know enough then about life in rebel prisons to fully appreciate their kindness. Every day on the arrival of the mail, one of them would bring in a late paper, stand up on a box and read the news. . . . In many other ways, such as procuring writing materials and forwarding letters for us, they manifested such kindly feeling as one honorable soldier will always manifest toward a brother soldier, enemy though he be, in misfortune."[2]

Grigsby said the return of knives, jewelry, watches, money, and other items collected on the prisoners' arrival surprised the men. None believed, he said, the promise that the valuables would be restored when the prisoners left Cahaba, although a Confederate officer made a list of what was taken from each. "Let it be said to their honor that they carried out their promise to the letter, that when we were (about to be) taken from Cahaba to Andersonville prison pen, they came in and returned every Cahaba prisoner the articles taken as shown by the list."[3]

Lieutenant Edmund E. Ryan, a law book salesman from Philadelphia who enlisted in the Seventeenth Illinois Infantry while living temporarily in Peoria, agreed with Grigsby about the treatment, if not about the food. "The officers and soldiers treat us as officers and true soldiers should treat prisoners of war," he wrote in his diary. Ryan, who arrived on February 21, 1864, was less pleased with other matters. He recorded the daily ration as a quart of corn meal and a quarter pound of meat. "Sometimes we receive a few cow peas which are not fit for man to eat." The men spent their time, he said, cooking, sleeping, reading, playing cards, singing, and "discussing the various subjects of the day." It was difficult to keep the prison clean, he said, and vermin constantly beset the men. "It is a hard, disagreeable life for a human being to live."[4]

Grigsby and Ryan were among the 660 men whom surgeon Whitfield reported to be in the prison just before the exodus of the enlisted men to Andersonville.[5] Ryan went to the officers' prison at Macon.

It should be noted that Ryan said the men spent part of their time reading. Castle Morgan was supplied abundantly with books of all types by Amanda Gardner, who lived in a house a few feet from the northwest corner of the stockade, helping to make the prison different from most Civil War prison camps. Men in Andersonville longed for something other than the Bible to read, while men in Cahaba had all they wished.[6]

Those in Castle Morgan were not better off in all things, however, than those in Andersonville, for they were more crowded. No official figures exist for the number of prisoners during the last months of the war, when it was most densely packed, but several sources place it at 3,000. These include Jesse Hawes, the 101st Ohio Infantry's history, John L. Walker, and Anna M. Gayle Fry, who lived in Cahaba. Colonel Chandler provided the last official figures, listing the prison population as 2,151 on October 16, 1864. When Henderson arranged Federal supplies for the prison two months later, the shipment included two thousand each of the major items, such as pants, shoes, and hats, and the same number of envelopes in which to mail letters home.[7] The prison remained in operation another several months, however.

No matter which figures are accepted, the crowding likely was the worst of any major Civil War prison. Surgeon Whitfield, in his report on March 31, 1864, said the warehouse walls, inside which the men were locked each night, enclosed 15,000 square feet. This would give 2,000 men 7.5 square feet of space each, and 3,000 men 5 square feet. Hawes placed it at 6 square feet. Without the bunks, which were arranged in tiers, the men would have had insufficient space for all to lie down at once on the sandy ground. Adding the maximum area enclosed by the stockade and its extension ordered by Colonel Chandler, only part of which was permitted the men during daylight and none during darkness, 2,000 would have no more than 17.5 square feet of space each, and 3,000 would have but 12. Andersonville, however, at its peak population of 32,899 in August 1864, still provided an average of 35.7 square feet.[8]

52   **The Men**

Vermin of all sorts assaulted the men of Castle Morgan: rats, lice, and muggers. The muggers were captured Union soldiers who preyed on their companions, banding together to steal and torment for profit and pleasure. But lack of food caused the most misery, for as the South's fortunes waned, so did those of the prisoners. The daily quart of meal and quarter pound of meat, which Lieutenant Ryan thought insufficient, dwindled by nearly all accounts to a pint or pint and a half of cornmeal and an occasional nibble of pork or beef, sometimes augmented with beans. The bread and meat that Colonel Chandler said was the basic diet in October 1864, was largely but a memory in the last months.

To keep going, the South resorted to a tax in kind, the collection of taxes in produce and goods rather than in paper money constantly declining in value. The tax came to be popularly known as "the government tithe." Captain J. J. Wheadon was in charge of subsistence at Cahaba and also collected the tithe. He therefore had to supply the prison and also gather the taxes in provisions due the Confederacy from the area's farms and plantations. His territory included three counties and part of a fourth, but while the number of prisoners grew by as much as five times in the last year, his territory increased not an inch, and he attempted to feed as many as 3,000 from the same sources used for the earlier 660.[9]

Preparation of the raw food the prisoners received presented another perplexing problem. Few tools and utensils were available, and the men had little with which to cut up the logs provided for firewood. They cooked in a small walled-in yard just outside the stockade, and the restricted ground was covered with small fires as men designated to cook for their squads were at work. With a population of more than two thousand and a cooking fire for each ten-man squad, from two hundred to three hundred fires were going at once. Sergeant Aldrich recalled, "The smoke was too thick to breathe, and one could not stay there long enough to bake his pone, but had to be relieved by some of the squad that remained inside of the walls."[10]

There is mild disagreement in prisoner memoirs, letters, and diaries about some of the food, but most agreed about the daily ration of cornmeal. The pint to a pint and a half per man was ground together with pieces of husk and cob. Hawes said he and his squad attempted to improve the cornmeal by making a sieve from half a canteen through which to sift it and remove the coarser particles. But they found too little was left, and the sieve was given up after two days. "Our intellects could understand that the coarse cob in our meal was of no more value than its bulk of sawdust, but our stomachs were carnal, obstinate, unreasonable."[11]

Men used every imaginable way to prepare the ground corn. It was browned and turned into "coffee," fried, boiled, mixed with bacon or beef, and even soaked in water until it soured and became "corn beer." It was augmented by a few ounces of bacon or beef, some said daily; others said it came only every two or three days. Sergeant Aldrich said this meat ration consisted of but a partial quarter of beef divided among a hundred men. Hawes said the meat usually was spoiled and he covered it for several hours with charcoal gathered from cooking fires, leaving it blackened but less violent to the nose. A small amount of salt came occasionally, along with pumpkins and a bit of lard. For eating utensils, the men sharpened sticks or carved crude wooden spoons. The best meals for some came at night. "As soon as I had gone to sleep I nearly always began to dream of being at home, and as soon as I would enter the house I at once went to the pantry and began to eat. Oh, what delightful lunches I used to get in those dream journeys to the house pantry!"[12]

John Walker enjoyed one fine meal at Cahaba with his friend, William M. Morrow, a fellow member of Company B, Fiftieth Ohio. At least it seemed fine then, and in his memory. He secured assignment to a detail loading machinery onto a steamboat and chatted with the civilian in charge of the loading, who also was from Ohio. When the work was done, the civilian slipped two Confederate dollars to Walker. He spent it on two sweet potatoes before returning to the prison. "That night Billy Morrow and I had a feast, the best meal we had had since our capture."[13]

Among the descriptions of the food in Castle Morgan during the war's last months, one strong dissent exists. Corporal Edwin Ford of Company D, Eighteenth Michigan Volunteer Infantry, wrote home to Hillsdale, Michigan, about a bounty of food. He said he was gaining weight. "We have plenty to eat—the rations we draw are meal, beef, rice, salt, lard, and occasionally flour," he wrote to his parents on December 8, 1864. "Some of the men are getting dinner—a soup of beef and rice, a first rate dish by the way, especially for a prisoner of war. This is no such prison as Andersonville is represented to be." He wrote again on January 24, this time to his sister, Mary A. Ford, also of Hillsdale. "I have plenty to eat and have an excellent appetite and weigh more than I ever did at home. That dont [sic] look much like starving." It was Ford who said the prisoners probably fared better than the inmates of any other Confederate prison.[14]

Corporal A. Lewis Jennings, Ford's companion and also a member of Company D of the Eighteenth Michigan, wrote home to Hillsdale, too, but without quite so much enthusiasm about his diet. "We have meal and bacon for food, and generally enough of it," he said in a letter to Mrs. E. K. Pennell on October 29.[15]

Ford's description of the food and conditions in the prison may have been intended in part to reassure his parents. It may have been also because he knew authorities censored his letters. All mail to and from prisoners had to be sent unsealed to ease its reading by the officers in charge.[16] This censorship is demonstrated by a letter dated March 31, 1864, from Captain Henderson to the Selma *Morning Reporter*. It appeared in the issue of April 2.

Mr. Editor: Before sending Federal prisoners' letters North by flag of truce, the duty devolves upon me of reading and approving what they write. From their correspondence I take from one letter the following extract:

"Dear Father: You cannot imagine how many homes we have destroyed (and some of them those of poor widows) in this last raid. When I was captured I ran through the picket lines, and was not hurt by the fire opened upon me. My horse was shot by a citizen as I passed his burnt dwelling. When my horse plunged forward and fell, I was slightly hurt. After I arose, three citizens stood by me with as many shotguns leveled at my head. They said I was the first Yankee that had fallen in their hands since their houses were burned and their families turned out to the mercy of the pitiless elements, and that they would make me suffer. Such had been the brutality of many of my comrades, that I could not ask for quarter. There was the wife of one of them, and three shivering hungry little children; their clothing and food had been burned or stolen by our cavalry, but they spared my life, the soldiers took charge of me, and I was well treated. I was sorry to be captured a few months before my term of enlistment expired. Since my capture I have seen more of the South and its slaves than I ever expected to see. Let no man, hereafter, speak to me about fighting to free negroes. The people of the South are humane, and the negroes well satisfied, until our army threw the firebrand of discontent into their midst. I took the oath, in good faith, to serve the United States three years. My time will soon be out, and I shall not re-enlist. I do not know whether I shall have a chance to see home or not when the election comes off this fall, but dear father, do all that you can to put the Democratic party in power. I think if this can be effected, the inhuman war will speedily end."

The above extract is similar in spirit to many other views which come under my notice.[17]

Discipline necessarily was rigorous for most of the men in Castle Morgan because of the many prisoners and few guards. A deadline, beyond which no prisoner dared venture without permission for fear of being shot, was several feet inside the stockade wall. Two sets of stairs led to the guards' walkway around the top of the stockade. One was at the western end of the north wall and the other was a few feet away on the west wall. The gate leading into the prison yard was between the stairs, in the northwest corner. At least two small cannon poked through holes in the north wall, positioned to sweep the whole interior. John Walker said there were three and "looking into these muzzles I could see the tin can which contained a charge of canister ready for any outbreak which might occur in the prison." Roll calls were held daily at 7:30 A.M. and 5 P.M., with all lights extinguished at 9 P.M., rules also enforced at other prisons.[18]

A ladder leaned against the stockade on the outside, near the northwest corner, and Lieutenant Colonel Jones used it to punish misbehaving prisoners. They were made to stand beneath it, grab a high rung, place their feet on a lower one and hang there for up to twenty minutes. "I have seen the boys so lame the next day that they could hardly walk," wrote Sergeant Aldrich.[19]

Restrictions were less harsh for some. Captured officers were paroled to live in the town on their pledge not to attempt to flee or to communicate with local residents except as necessary. Colonel Chandler reported ten of these at Cahaba in October 1864, saying that, "Living in quarters

The Men 57

furnished them in the town, they are much more comfortable than the other prisoners, and express themselves perfectly satisfied with their treatment." Lieutenant E. J. Squire of the 101st Ohio Infantry, was invited to inspect the prison books and found nothing amiss.[20]

Often the men were busy at tasks other than the usual cooking, fighting lice and rats, cleaning the prison, and planning escapes. Details went outside to gather wood and do other work. Members of the Eighteenth Michigan Band furnished music for guard mount and parades. A number of men from the 115th Ohio served as carpenters, and two of the clerks in the prison office were Union soldiers. Twenty and more men at a time worked as attendants in the prison hospital. Private D. W. Garber of Company E, 102nd Ohio Volunteer Infantry, entertained himself by skillfully carving beautiful brooches from mussel shells obtained from the river.[21]

Dry firewood was almost as precious as food. John Walker said the amount permitted "was what split wood one man could carry on one arm," and had to last "some eight or ten days." Perry S. Summerville quickly discovered the value of wood. He was a member of Company K, Second Indiana Cavalry, and was with a forage detail near Stilesborough, Georgia, on September 13, 1864, when Confederates attacked. He fell as he leaped from his wagon, and a wheel rolled over his right leg, breaking it. Surgeons provided him with crutches before sending him to Cahaba. His leg grew worse, however, and he stayed in the prison hospital until November 14. While there he made a knife from a piece of iron hoop, which he used later in the stockade to trim wood for fuel. He slept with his head on his crutches to safeguard them, but soon resorted to carving pieces from one to start his fires. Soon that crutch was gone, and he began turning the other into tinder as well, a bit at the time. One night he failed to rest his head on the remainder, and "some fellow stole it with which to cook his breakfast."[22]

Stephen M. Gaston of Company K, Ninth Indiana Cavalry, was one of the youngest captives of the war. He was but thirteen when he enlisted, fourteen when taken by Confederate cavalry in north Alabama and put into Castle Morgan, and only four months into his fifteenth year when released. That he was permitted to enlist at such a tender age was unusual, of course, but about three hundred boys of thirteen talked their way past recruiters and onto the rolls of the Union army.[23]

Escape attempts were many and most failed. Jesse Hawes and two others fled by squeezing under the flooring of the water closet and along the ditch that drained it, then climbing over the stockade wall at a point where it consisted only of thin poles permitting flow of the water to the river. A companion distracted the nearest guard. The men ran and walked many miles toward Pensacola, Florida, which was held by the Union, but a slave spotted them and reported to his master. The plantation owner and his overseer tracked them down with hounds and returned them to Cahaba.[24]

George A. Tod, who enlisted as a drummer in Company I of the Thirty-second Iowa Infantry while only sixteen, was in the prison in April 1864, when a group tunneled out. It is unclear from his account how many were involved, but there were at least twelve. The tunnel began in the dirt floor of the warehouse, went deep enough to pass beneath the stockade, and ended in the steep river bank. The escapees waited until dark to push through the final inches of dirt, and managed to cross the Alabama River. They reached a planter's stable, where they stole horses and mules, and covered about sixty miles before being captured. This may have been the same escape related by Aldrich, who said the recaptured men "were put back into prison with the rest of us, with ball and chain, and they were punished and suffered for months in that way." Such accounts are supported by existence of a depression on the river bank which appears to be the exit of an escape tunnel.[25]

Tod said another fifteen got away by cutting through the brick wall of the warehouse and removing a stockade post. They too were recaptured and two who had escaped several times were placed in irons.[26]

George F. Robinson, Company C, Second Michigan Cavalry, was serving his third enlistment when taken at Shoal Creek, Alabama, on November 5, 1864, and was as persistent in his escape attempts as he was in remaining a soldier. He was imprisoned first at Meridian, but tunneled out and covered sixty miles before recapture. He then was put on the train for Selma. About six miles past Demopolis, he and a fellow trooper of the same unit, John Corliss, jumped from the car window while the train was traveling. "I did not stop immediately but rolled along after the train quite a distance," Robinson remembered. He suffered a "big hole cut in my head," but he and Corliss eluded pursuers for five days and nights in weather so cold the trees wore icicles. "We were almost starved and nearly frozen. Had nothing to eat but raw corn, and no fire, and wallowing through the swamp in the month of December."

Robinson said he and Corliss were taken to Castle Morgan, where they escaped again after several weeks, cutting a hole through the stockade. They fled to the north of Selma before capture. They were locked in a building in Selma, and escaped from that by chiseling through a brick wall "with an old knife and a piece of round iron—I think a piece of poker." But they were caught again and returned to Cahaba.[27]

By the prisoners' accounts, just the vermin were enough to make a man attempt to escape. Perry Summerville said that after his first night in Castle Morgan he was so covered with lice "my clothes looked more like pepper and salt goods than blue." John Walker remembered that one of the first things he saw on entering the prison was a man about to receive a rough scrubbing and a thorough hair cut by a committee which thought him negligent of his person. "I can never forget the sight of his head. It was one solid mass of corruption, covered with vermin, and actually 'alive,' as the scalp literally swayed from side to side." Jesse Hawes, who found the lice the most disgusting of pests, said, "they crawled upon our clothing by day . . . crawled over our bodies, into the ears, even into the nostrils and mouths by night." Sergeant Aldrich said the prisoners called the lice *graybacks*, the same name they used for Confederate soldiers, and most of the men cut their hair as short as possible to control the vermin. "To feel them crawl and bite was additional creeping torture," he wrote.[28]

Rats added their torments. "Hardly would I get asleep when one or more would be snuffing about some portion of my body," Hawes said. "The same experience was often repeated: go to the bed of sand at nine P.M., dream of food till one or two A.M., awake, go to the water barrel, drink and return to sleep again, if the rats would permit sleep."[29]

Little clothing remained for some of the men after they bartered for extra food from the guards. Sergeant Aldrich said some wore only drawers and the sun tanned them nearly black. "I asked one of them what had become of his clothes and he said he had sold them to the guard for something to eat."[30]

Tod, the drummer boy, was small even for his age and apparently looked even younger. That brought certain benefits before he arrived at Cahaba. According to his account, first published in an Iowa newspaper, the Fort Dodge *North West*, on January 10 and January 17, 1865, he was captured on February 4, 1864, while serving with Sherman in Mississippi. He straggled on the second day of a march out of Vicksburg because his knapsack was too heavy for his small frame, and Confederate soldiers scouting the column grabbed him. They took him to Jackson. Then he began a long walk to Morton under guard with other prisoners. On the way, a regiment of Confederate cavalry joined the procession, and one of the officers called out, "Hello, little fellow, ain't you most tired out?" A trooper rode up and lifted Tod onto his horse, and the boy had a ride the rest of the day. The following morning at Morton, a sympathetic Confederate sergeant gave Tod and his fellow prisoners ten dollars with which to buy food. They spent it at the train station for biscuits at four for a dollar, and sweet potato pies at a dollar each. They rode the train to Selma and a steamboat from there to Cahaba. Their travels were not over, however. They were with Melvin Grigsby and the others transferred to Andersonville two months later.[31]

In September 1864, with too many men and not enough of anything for them, Captain Henderson proposed a special exchange of about 350 of Cahaba's inmates, members of the Federal Sixteenth Army Corps, for their equivalent in captured southerners from the Confederacy's Department of Alabama, Mississippi and East Louisiana. Union Major General Cadwallader C. Washburn, commanding the District of West Tennessee, sent the proposal to Colonel William Hoffman, commissary general of prisoners, saying he had no Confederates with which to make the exchange and requesting that they be provided from prisons in the North. "At present our prisoners are in good health," he said, "but they are sadly in need of clothing, and as cold weather comes on their sufferings will be great and probably much sickness will ensue." He said no colored soldiers were involved, but that a white major of colored artillery was at Cahaba "and very badly treated, but it is proposed to exchange him with the rest." Washburn said the matter was "a question of humanity," and the North would not be injured "as the soldiers are now in condition to be fit for duty at once." Colonel Hoffman referred the proposal to Lieutenant General Grant and the exchange was not made.[32] There is no further mention of the mistreated major. His fate is not known, but no major was included on the official lists of those who died at Cahaba.

With the failure of the exchange effort, Henderson and Washburn negotiated the steamboat load of supplies for the Cahaba prisoners. That, too, almost failed. Washburn's superiors required that a Union officer accompany the material to see that it went to the prisoners and not the Confederacy, but Major General Maury of the District of the Gulf, refused to permit a Federal officer to cross his lines. Henderson and Washburn managed to overcome the problem by agreeing that officers of Washburn's staff captured by General Nathan Bedford Forrest, and therefore prisoners themselves, could distribute the supplies. Thus it was that in December 1864 a steamboat of mercy passed under flag of truce up the Alabama River to Castle Morgan, delivering two thousand coats and hats; two thousand pairs of pants, drawers, and shoes; four thousand pairs of socks; fifteen hundred blankets; medicine, envelopes, and writing paper; and a hundred mess tins.[33]

The effort to equip the men went awry, however. What they wanted most was food, and Captain Henderson said they bartered away their new items to the guards. When the food was gone, they were left about as they were before the shipment from the North, hungry and "shivering in scanty clothing and ragged blankets in a climate particularly severe in the transition period from winter to spring."[34] But then that spring would be the war's last.

The Men 63

5
The Hospital and
the Toll

In the days of Cahaba's early prominence and prosperity, a favorite stopping place for the wealthy was the Bell Tavern hotel on Vine Street, the main business street of the town. The civic and amusement center, the hotel attracted well-to-do gentlemen, politicians, planters, and travelers awaiting a steamboat. They gathered there to drink, play billiards or high-stakes poker, and to discuss politics. A Cahaba tradition holds that the great banquet honoring LaFayette in 1825, when Cahaba was the state capital, was held there. It remained an important place of civic affairs and entertainment through the early 1850s, when superseded by the new Saltmarsh Hall, and was the scene of many grand balls. Then in 1863 the rambling old two-story frame building, painted white, its windows shaded with green blinds, became important again, but for a different reason. The Confederacy commandeered it as a hospital to serve alike southern soldier and Union prisoner. The long ballroom, where once danced the wealthy gentleman and southern belle, became filled with long rows of white cots occupied by suffering men. Only part of the hotel, about two blocks from the prison, was used at first, but later the hospital was expanded to include all the building and part of a house as the number of patients soared to more than two hundred at a time.[1]

Louis E. Profilet was the chief surgeon. He did not labor alone, of course. Isaiah H. White also was a surgeon in Bell Tavern, along with other surgeons and assistant surgeons. The prison surgeon, R. H. Whitfield, worked in the hospital as well. Profilet enlisted the aid, too, of up to twenty-two Federal prisoners at a time detailed as attendants. The hospital records for the first week in December 1864 list twenty-five other helpers, including nurses, matrons, the steward, cooks, and laundresses. Some of them were slaves, and a reminder is on the record for January 12, 1865: "Have Tom return to his master." A week later, however, Tom was back at Bell Tavern, and the steward, who kept the surgeons' records, jotted down, "Tom hired as nurse." Another helper decided to change uniforms and left on January 18, the day before Tom's return. The record-keeper noted, "Charles Schallon. Yankee Deserter Hired As Cook. Enlisted in CSA. Left this morning." The townspeople helped, too. The ladies of Cahaba formed a sewing club to make Confederate uniforms and each week appointed some of their number to nurse in the hospital.[2]

It is impossible to say with precision how many men died while imprisoned at Cahaba. Confederate records list 142, Federal records 147. However, 224 depressions indicating graves lie in the nearby cemetery where Union prisoners buried their dead. The graves were dug up after the war and the disinterred carried to the national cemetery at Marietta, Georgia, but those reburied totaled only 162. A few of them were listed as possibly having died elsewhere and their bodies carried to Cahaba as a convenient burial place or, perhaps, so they might rest with their fellow soldiers. In addition, workmen discovered a grave con-

The Hospital and the Toll 65

An artist's depiction of Castle Morgan shortly after the war. However, it shows neither the brick construction of the warehouse nor the wooden stockade. (Benson J. Lossing, *Pictorial History of the Civil War in the United States of America*, Volume 3, Hartford, 1877; The University of Alabama Special Collections Library)

taining human bones and Federal uniform buttons on the riverbank at the prison site in the early 1980s. They reburied bones and buttons where they found them.[3]

Castle Morgan probably held about 5,000 men altogether, including 1,500 transferred early to Andersonville, 400 sent to Meridian, more than 100 who went to Savannah for exchange, and the almost 3,000 who remained to the end. If one accepts 225 as the total of deaths—the number of depressions in the former cemetery and the grave on the riverbank—and 5,000 as the total number of inmates, the death rate was less than 5 percent. If the Federal total of 147 is used, death claimed only about 3 percent. In either case, well might Lewis Day write, "This was one of the

66 **The Hospital and the Toll**

exceedingly well-conducted prisons in the whole South." That does not say that exposure, danger, and hunger were absent. Surely the men suffered. It appears, however, that they died in unusually small numbers for prisoners during a war in which the average soldier's chance of not returning home was a horrifying one in four. It should be recalled that the overall prison camp death percentage was 15.5 in the South and 12 percent in the North.[4]

There is no way to determine whether the hospital death register included men killed or who died of disease inside the prison, since they never made it to Bell Tavern. Such deaths would explain the difference of almost ninety in the totals from the hospital records and the number of graves in the cemetery. Sergeant Aldrich claimed he saw as many as ten Union men die in one night. "The rebs would come in with the stretchers and four or five of our boys would help them carry our dead comrades out and bury them."[5] However, no other prisoner mentioned so high a toll within the prison.

One other shred of information warrants consideration. The Montgomery *Advertiser* carried an item on March 14, 1894, which it said was reprinted from the Mobile *Register*. It listed boats lost on the Alabama River from 1865 to 1894 as recalled by "an old Alabama river pilot." It included a steamboat named the *Autauga*, which supposedly sank near Montgomery while carrying the corpses of Union dead from Selma to Montgomery. The recent rediscovery of the report, reprinted also in *Transactions of the Alabama Historical Society, 1897–1898,*[6] drew the attention of those interested in Cahaba Federal Prison, but there is no evidence the bodies said to be on the *Autauga* came from Cahaba. The item did not mention the prison. It gave no date for the sinking, although the *Autauga* was first on the list of lost boats. It has not been possible to learn further details of the *Autauga* or to even prove that a boat by that name existed. However, such an incident could account for the discrepancy between the number of gravelike depressions in the cemetery and the number of bodies reburied at Marietta.

The Federal government appeared satisfied after the war that all who died at Cahaba had been counted. Major General E. A. Hitchcock, commissary general of prisoners, reported to Secretary of War Edwin M. Stanton on July 18, 1866, that fatality lists from most prison stations in the South were incomplete "with the exception of those received from Andersonville, Ga., Salisbury, N.C., Cahaba, Ala., and Danville, Va."[7] None of the figures, of course, include those who died after leaving Cahaba for Andersonville or elsewhere of injury or disease that originated in Cahaba.

It is always possible that more Federal men died at Cahaba than the records or the graves in the cemetery indicate, that uncounted bodies were thrown in the river, or that some unknown or forgotten burial place lies overgrown in the woods. However, no evidence has been found to support such a possibility, and it is likely that the death toll was around 225.

The Cahaba hospital records, from which the figure of 142 is taken, show the first Union soldier to die was Private Alfred Douglas of Company I, Sixty-sixth Illinois, a victim of *febris typhoides*, or typhoid fever. He died on December 28, 1863. A member of the First Alabama Cavalry, a Union regiment, was next, Private David Reid of Company E succumbing to what the surgeons said was pneumonia on January 26, 1864. The surgeons were tardy in starting their record-keeping, since they first listed Reid as Number One on a register entitled "Deaths among [sic] Federals," but later apparently remembered Private Douglas and added his name. That they included the earlier death after beginning the register shows a certain dedication to accuracy.

The third victim died on the same day as Reid and also was identified as a member of a Union regiment from a southern state, the First Mississippi Marines. Private William Dailey of Company I, the surgeons noted, suffered *vulnus sclopeticum,* a gunshot wound. The term, used by all doctors and surgeons of the time, was taken from the Latin *vulnus* for wound and *sclopus* for gun.

A Roll of Honor issued by the U.S. Army Quartermaster General in 1868 is the source for the Federal total of 147 deaths.[9] It was based in part on the Confederate records but also included all other information the government could gather. It listed ten deaths from gunshots or other injuries which could have been inflicted either by guards or suffered before or during capture. Reid's fatal pneumonia, according to this roll, resulted from a wound. It is suspicious that the first two deaths by wounds were on the same day and involved Alabama and Mississippi men serving the Union cause, but they were the only such men identified as dying of wounds, and the records of neither side say when or where any of the injuries occurred. The fatal shootings of Privates N. D. Riggen and John Rumels also merit extra notice. According to the Federal report, both were members of Company I, Seventh Illinois, and both died on November 16, 1864. The records from Bell Tavern, however, said Rumels was a member of Company I, Fifty-ninth Illinois, who died on February 11, 1865, of debilitation.

The others included on the Federal report as dying of wounds were, with date of death, Corporal John H. Ballard, Company H, Third Pennsylvania, January 4, 1865; Private Frederick Berney, Company G, Third Wisconsin, August 14, 1864; Private Thomas Carter, Company C, 120th Illinois, October 29, 1864; Private C. W. Eddy, Company K, Seventh Missouri, April 5, 1864; Private Benjamin J. Simail, Company F, Twenty-first Missouri, October 1,

1864; and Private L. C. Todd, Company E, Third Michigan Cavalry, September 22, 1864. The cause of death of Reid and Eddy was listed only as "wound." The rest were gunshot victims.[10]

The surgeons in Bell Tavern did not include Eddy and Todd on their death list, but recorded one the Union missed: Private L. C. Kidd of Company E, Third Michigan Cavalry, who died of a gunshot wound on September 22, 1864. Corporal Ballard, included as a member of the Third Pennsylvania on the government list, belonged to the Third Tennessee Cavalry, according to the surgeons.

With the exceptions noted, the records of the surgeons and the Federal government agree on those who died in Bell Tavern of wounds, indicating at least eleven Federal soldiers were such victims during the nearly two years Castle Morgan was open, with some of the wounds doubtlessly occurring in combat before capture. Indeed, Colonel Chandler, the inspector general who filed the report on Castle Morgan and the hospital on October 16, 1864, said that forty wounded men then were in the prison.[11]

It is probable that some of the deaths came at the hands of guards, and the stories of survivors include several incidents involving Lieutenant Colonel Jones's ill-trained men. None of the survivors, however, fully identified victims, and it is not possible to match them with certainty to the lists of the dead. Jesse Hawes charged that two guards, one a boy of sixteen, killed three prisoners each with rifle or bayonet. Hawes gave the name of the older Confederate only as Hankins, "one of the most savage rascals we had to guard us." The hospital records confirm the existence of a guard by that name. Private F. M. Hankins was treated for a fever and returned to duty on January 30, 1865. There is no way to know, of course, but it could be that Private Eddy was the young soldier Hawes identified as "Teddy" who, according to Hawes, was fa-

70 **The Hospital and the Toll**

tally shot in the back by Hankins for pausing a moment in the doorway between the cook yard and the warehouse.[12]

George Tod, the drummer boy from Iowa, said a new guard was heard to say on his first morning of duty that "he would kill a Yankee before night." The man, said Tod, did not speak idly. "During the day one of the prisoners stood looking through the crack in the door, when this guard, without a word, drew up his musket and shot him dead." Sergeant Aldrich wrote that a sandy-haired young Confederate was on guard at the door of the cook yard and stopped a prisoner reentering the warehouse after preparing cornmeal mush in a pail suspended over a fire by a piece of wood. The guard told the prisoner he could not take the wood back inside. "The man halted and looked around, but not knowing that the guard meant him or referred to the little stick in question, started on, whereupon the guard struck him in the back with the bayonet and ran it through his body. He fell to the ground and soon breathed his last."[13]

One of the more significant facts to be noted from the Federal Roll of Honor is that only two men died of scorbutus, or scurvy, that disease caused by a lack of vitamin C in the diet which killed so many at Andersonville, including eighty-two just in May and June of 1864. This could indicate either that more vegetables were provided than the prisoners claimed, which from most reports appears unlikely, or that the hospital enjoyed sufficient provisions to arrest the disease. The surgeons did not list scorbutus among diseases treated, but Colonel Chandler said in his report that "there are a number of cases of scurvy."[14]

Alonzo A. Van Vlack, Company F, Eighteenth Michigan Volunteer Infantry, who said he "suffered everything but death," at Cahaba, claimed "my legs were one raw sore from my knees down to my feet with scurvy." The records do not indicate that he was treated at the hospital, however. Those the Roll of Honor listed as dying of scurvy were Private P. Coilen, Company B, Fourth United States, March 20, 1864, and Private J. W. Randolph, Company G, Sixth Illinois, March 28, 1864. The hospital records do not mention Private Coilen, and say that Private Randolph died of pneumonia.[15]

Another of the interesting aspects in the records is the absence of a killing epidemic of any one disease, which may be surprising in such crowded conditions, although several men had typhoid fever and many suffered measles. Not surprisingly, pneumonia and disorders of the digestive tract were by far the biggest killers among the Federals. The surgeons recorded forty-one pneumonia deaths, including those of Reid and Randolph, who the Union report said died of gunshot and scurvy respectively. The cases of these two may not have been fabrications by the Confederate surgeons. It was not uncommon for the weakness brought on by injury or disease to result in pneumonia, which then produced death.

The surgeons also reported thirty-nine deaths by diarrhea and dysentery. Neither the surgeons nor the Federal roll included any deaths from gangrene, a scourge at Andersonville. Only one case was treated in Bell Tavern, that of Private Alpha Gerei of Company C, 114th Illinois. The treatment is not listed, but one remedy was the introduction of maggots, fly larvae which release a chemical enhancing the digestion of dead flesh so they may consume it more efficiently. By removing the decayed material, they promote growth of new and healthy tissue. Napoleon's surgeons first discovered their usefulness, and they were employed through World War I. Whatever the treatment, Gerei was well enough to be returned to the prison on October 19, 1864.[16]

72   **The Hospital and the Toll**

Seven of the Union victims of Cahaba Federal Prison were civilians.[17] Two were identified as government employees, N. H. Edwards dying on January 8, 1864, of chronic diarrhea, and Henry Fairchilds [sic] on September 8, 1864, of what was diagnosed as congestion and fever. Their home states were not listed either in Confederate records or on the Roll of Honor. Martin U. Hardy and Alvin Emery were identified only as citizens of Illinois. Hardy died on September 25, 1864, also of congestion and fever, and Emery on October 8, 1864, of *febris remittens*, remittent fever. John Lawdon and G. D. Smith were citizens of New York. Lawdon died on January 2, 1865, of an inflammation of the bowels, and Smith on January 11, 1865, of consumption. William G. Watson, a citizen of Maine, succumbed to diarrhea on February 11, 1865. How these people came to be prisoners at Cahaba is not discernible from the surviving records, but it was not unusual for either side to imprison employees of the opposing government or civilians, such as sutlers, found with captured soldiers.

The surgeons also recorded the deaths of twenty-one Confederate soldiers from January 4, 1864, through March 16, 1865. Ten of them possibly were prison guards, judging from their units. Causes of death included three by pneumonia, three by typhoid fever, five by congestion and fever, and three by diarrhea or dysentery. None died of wounds. The first was Private Robert M. Gardner of Company L, Third Kentucky, a victim of *rheumatismus*, or some form of rheumatic disease, and the last one Private Lewis Larkin, a guard, who died of congestion and fever.[18]

Reasons for the comparatively small death toll at Cahaba Federal Prison and in Bell Tavern may be speculated on with some confidence. The confined area of Castle Morgan, however unpleasant, may have been beneficial, small spaces being easier to clean. Surgeon Whitfield complained early about the accumulation of rubbish and filth, and this may have resulted in improvement. Clearly there were many hands to do the work. In addition, the prisoners were provided toilet facilities that carried fecal matter to the river to be diluted and washed away downstream. They drank clean water straight from a natural spring, at least after surgeon Whitfield complained and pipes replaced the open ditch. At Andersonville, however, the prisoners had twenty-six acres to police, and the lack of proper facilities led thousands to defecate in a swamp occupying three and a half acres in the center of the prison, producing a rich source of disease and polluting the water supply.[19]

Another blessing enjoyed by the men of Castle Morgan and Bell Tavern was nearby sources of medicine, and apparently no serious shortage occurred. Demopolis and Montgomery were the two depots for medical supplies in the state, and Cahaba sat approximately midway between them. Demopolis is only forty miles from Selma, then a day's round trip to the west on the Alabama and Mississippi Rivers Railroad. Montgomery is about an equal distance to the east and was connected by steamboat, if not by rail. Surgeon E. H. C. Bailey, in charge of the Demopolis depot, reported in October 1864 that his stock included 1,966 ounces of quinine sulfate, 245 drams of morphine sulfate, and 34 pounds of chloroform. Additionally, the steamboat that arrived in December 1864 with Union supplies for the prisoners, brought "a sufficient amount of medicines to supply said prisoners."[20]

The prison hospital was in a building originally used as a hotel and perhaps constructed with comfort in mind. It likely was as clean and comfortable as could be provided in such an area under wartime conditions, and was well staffed. Dr. Whitfield's complaints are evidence of the surgeons' concern, and there is no indication of hospital care favoring the Rebel over the Yankee.

Despite certain obvious benefits that kept the death toll low, the men were not provided proper clothing, warmth, and protection from the elements by all accounts. Vermin were uncontrollable and rampant; food scant, coarse, and ill-preserved. These things contributed to pneumonia, diarrhea, and dysentery being the major killers.

Perry Summerville, the youth with the broken leg who used wood trimmed from his crutches to kindle his fires, wrote that he asked to be released early from the hospital because "to see the dead carried out every morning was too much for me." He was returned from Bell Tavern to the prison on November 14, 1864, and the surgeons' records show that during that week no fewer than twelve Union men died. The worst day was November 12, two days before Private Summerville's release, when he would have seen four bodies removed.[21] At least one prisoner died each day from November 7 through November 14, Summerville's last week in the hospital, and during the period November 1864 through April 1865 the surgeons recorded that death visited in Bell Tavern on seventy-five days, never, however, claiming more than four men on one day.

The debility and diseases diagnosed in the hospital ran the gamut of things that can go wrong with the human body, from hemorrhoids to ulcers, from a Confederate's plain nostalgia to vertigo, from anthrax to tonsillitis. One case of venereal disease was reported, a member of the Union's Seventh Kentucky Cavalry requiring treatment for gonorrhea. Private John Roberts of Company A, Ninth Illinois, was treated for frostbite and returned to the prison on January 26, 1865. This happened during a time when, according to Sergeant Aldrich, "the temperature began to fall, and kept going down and down below the freezing point . . . the rain changed to sleet and then to snow, while a keen and bitter wind chilled the very marrow in our poorly covered bones."[22]

Jesse Hawes did not mention it in his book, but he also was a patient at the hospital. This makes amusing his observation that, "A very fair hospital was said to have been in Cahaba. This statement is not doubted." The surgeons first diagnosed and recorded his problem as "nothing," but then added *rheumatismus acutus*. Perhaps his trouble really was "nothing" and he was embarrassed, since at the time he wrote he was himself a doctor. However, it should be noted that Hawes was dismissed from Bell Tavern and returned to the prison on January 29, 1865. This was a few days after Private Roberts's treatment for frostbite, the time Sergeant Aldrich said was so cold. Hawes could not be faulted if he sought a warm place, and maybe the cold made his joints ache. Bell Tavern certainly was kept warm. Records show that surgeon Profilet kept ten fires going and requisitioned twenty cords of wood at a time.[23]

Colonel Chandler said in the portion of his report dealing with the hospital that "this building is kept in good police, but the accommodations are entirely inadequate for the present number of patients." He said that 69 prisoners then were hospitalized and another 75 would have been had there been adequate space. He suggested that all Bell Tavern be taken over and that a contiguous house be used as well. The extra space was added, and by November 11 the surgeons were tending 209 men, 156 Federals and 53 Confederates. Relief for 110 of the sick or wounded Federal patients came on November 22 when they were released to be sent to Savannah for a special exchange, leaving behind 34 hospitalized companions.[24]

The hospital population remained below a hundred until December 4, when 102 patients were reported. By January 1865 the sick or wounded men in Bell Tavern totaled 225.

The number peaked at 232 on February 10, including 173 Federals, possibly reflecting both winter weather and the dismal state of southern resources during the last weeks of the war. On March 14 the surgeons released 106 hospitalized Union men so they could start home with their companions in Castle Morgan in the renewal of regular prisoner exchanges finally arranged, leaving 80 Federals still too sick or hurt to travel. The number of those hospitalized steadily declined thereafter until only 9 patients remained on May 2, all of them Confederates. The entry for that date is the last one in the hospital records.[25]

The last Union soldier left in Cahaba as a prisoner also was the last to die. Private Samuel Cooke, Company H, Fourth Kentucky, became Number 142 on the hospital death register. He succumbed to chronic diarrhea on April 28, 1865.[26] He did not live long enough to know about the *Sultana*, that more than a thousand of his companions from Castle Morgan had died just the day before on the Mississippi River while bound at last for home.

Several hundred yards west of the prison site, a small clearing lies adjacent to the weed-grown, neglected cemetery which served the town in its earliest years. The little clearing, well tended and marked off by posts strung with heavy cable, is the place where the Union dead were buried. A private citizen came upon the tiny cemetery late in the 1970s and discovered the 224 unmarked shallow depressions of the right size to be graves. Possibly unaware that the Union bodies had been moved to Marietta, he arranged with a member of the Congress for delivery of small, flat gravestones such as used in U.S. military cemeteries. The stones were engraved with names from the Roll of Honor and placed without regard to who might be buried where. When the well-intentioned citizen found he had more depressions than names, he placed stones saying Unknown U.S. Soldier, Civil War. It is probable, however, that only one Union soldier still lies at Cahaba. He lies alone and unidentified next to the Alabama River a few feet from where the prison stood, although there could be other lonely burial places yet unfound. At the Marietta National Cemetery, though, are the graves of 76 Cahaba victims identified by name together with 86 others whose bodies could not be identified when removed from the little cemetery at Cahaba. The remains of these rest beneath stones that silently repeat: Unknown U.S. Soldier, Civil War.[27]

6
Amanda and Belle

The men inside Cahaba Federal Prison had a friend outside in Amanda Gardner. Her resources were meager and her influence in the prison limited, but she did what she could, and many of the men remembered. Among them was Melvin Grigsby who traveled from South Dakota nearly twenty years after the war just to see Amanda and her daughter, Anabelle, whom the prisoners knew as Belle. He benefited from their kindnesses while locked up in Castle Morgan but communicated with them only through notes, and saw them for the first time on his long trip back.[1]

Mrs. Gardner lived in a house only a few yards from the northwestern corner of the stockade, on Lot Number Six; the back of her house was not more than thirty feet from the stockade.[2] Mrs. Gardner could hear and see much that occurred at Castle Morgan.

She lost a son in Confederate service early in the war, before there was a prison in Cahaba, and another son neared military age who might also be summoned to battle.[3] Thus she had as much reason as anyone in the town to dislike Union soldiers. But Amanda responded with kindness where she found misery, even when the miserable wore enemy blue.

Amanda and her husband, Eldridge, moved from Georgia to Cahaba in 1841, when he was thirty-three and she was twenty-four. Their first child, Elizabeth, was born in Cahaba on July 1, 1841, and was followed by five more. Elizabeth also was the first of the Gardner children to die, and was not quite fifteen when the family carried her remains to the cemetery at the southwestern edge of town in February 1856.[4] Her grave still may be found in the wide shade of the ancient oaks and fragrant magnolias draped with Spanish moss that make the place seem forever quiet and without time. The stone marking the grave is cracked and worn by the weather of more than a century and a quarter, but it was elaborately inscribed and the words remain distinct. They give her name as Lizzie and her birth and death dates. They mourn: "Oh! Shall a murmur escape from our breast; do you ask how she lived; she set heaven before her. Do you ask how she died; in the faith of the blessed."

John Moseley was the census taker in those days, and in 1860 he recorded that a family of seven lived in the rented house then owned by J. R. Sommerville, a merchant, and later owned for about two years by the same Colonel Hill who built the warehouse.[5] Eldridge then was fifty-two and Amanda forty-three. The oldest child, John, seventeen, was a clerk. Next came William, twelve, mistakenly listed by Moseley as a girl named Willie; followed by Anabelle, nine; Emma, six; and Alice, one. Eldridge gave his profession as grocer in the 1850 census, but now said he was a railroad contractor, suggesting he helped build the Cahaba, Marion and Greensborough whose tracks ran right past the side of his house down Capitol Street to the Alabama River. Eldridge did not report owning any real estate or slaves to Moseley, and listed the value of his personal estate at five hundred dollars.

Alice, the baby, followed her older sister to the little cemetery sometime before 1870. Her gravestone perhaps suggests the poverty that arrived with the Civil War and loss of the railroad, for it is marked simply "Alice." No dates are given, but she was not included in the family by the 1870 census, the first after the war.[6] The remains of the two girls, sisters who shared none of the same years and thus never met, lie side-by-side in the shade and the timeless quiet.

The war was not very old when Amanda and Eldridge mourned a son as well. Clerk John Gardner answered his state's call for troops before there was a Confederacy. On January 14, 1861, he was elected fourth corporal of the Cahaba Rifles. Alabama had seceded just three days before, and the Confederate government had yet to be organized as it would be at Montgomery about forty miles to the east and also on the Alabama River. Although already a corporal, John, then eighteen, was not officially enlisted until April 10, 1861, by Captain Christopher C. Pegues, a lawyer and commander of the Cahaba Rifles.[7] The first shots of the war were fired at Fort Sumter two days after John Gardner became a Confederate soldier. He was the eighth enlisted man on the company roster, and would be one of the first to fall in battle.

The Cahaba Rifles were accepted into the service of the Confederate States of America on April 16, 1861, and became Company F of the Fifth Alabama Regiment. The unit went first to Pensacola but left there almost immediately for Virginia. It was part of General Richard Ewell's brigade at First Manassas and was on the field but not engaged. The Rifles' first battle losses came on May 31, 1862, at Seven Pines, when the southern army of General Joseph E. Johnston stopped retreating and lashed back at General George

B. McClellan's army trying to break into Richmond. Johnston was wounded that day, and General R. E. Lee succeeded to command. At least six Cahaba men were killed and another mortally wounded. Among the six was Corporal John A. Gardner, nineteen, a soldier for just over a year, killed in his first battle.[8] His remains were not returned to lie next to his sisters in the shade. Those who fell at Seven Pines remained there.

The war struck hard at Cahaba. The records are incomplete, but of the 180 men on the rolls of the Rifles, at least 64 died in combat or of disease. Captain Pegues, who formed the unit and made a soldier of Corporal Gardner, became a colonel and adjutant of the Fifth Alabama, but did not long survive Gardner. He was mortally wounded at Gaines's Mill not quite a month after Seven Pines. He left a wife, two sons, and two daughters, ranging in age from four to thirteen.[9]

With her son dead on a Virginia battlefield and another son nearly old enough for war, with so many of her neighbors gone never to return and grief a visitor in so many Cahaba homes, Mrs. Gardner might have felt differently and behaved differently toward the prisoners in Castle Morgan. But she did not nurse sorrow with resentment.

Melvin Grigsby returned in April 1884, in part because of Belle, for in those days of imprisonment he had become infatuated with her through notes they exchanged, at least infatuated with the idea of her, since he had not seen her. He did not know that at the time he longed for a glimpse of her, she was a girl of thirteen.

On his trip back to Cahaba, he went first to Castle Morgan to see the prison again. He was disappointed. "There was nothing there, not even a brick or stone, nothing but a rank growth of weeds to mark the place where the old prison warehouse stood." He found George Brenner, who had been one of the guards. Brenner then owned and occupied the house in which the Gardners had lived, having bought it from Colonel Hill early in 1864, and told Grigsby where to find the Gardners.[10]

Amanda and Belle occupied a rented house in Selma, and Belle worked as a dressmaker to support her mother. Amanda then was sixty-seven and Belle thirty-three. Grigsby does not tell us what became of the rest of the family, and did not write his impression of Belle. He said of Amanda, "She is of good family and in every sense a lady of culture and refinement. She is a fluent talker and uses elegant language." He said Mrs. Gardner "was during the war, and still is for that matter, a thorough rebel. That is, she believed the South was right and still believes so."[11]

Mrs. Gardner told Grigsby she was moved to pity by the condition of the prisoners in Castle Morgan despite her southern sentiments. Soon after the prison opened she began sending gifts of food, and almost daily a few potatoes, peas, green beans, corn, and other vegetables were passed through a small hole in the stockade. She nursed some of the sick in her home and sent to the prison what medicines she found in the town. She sent all the clothing and bedding she could spare to the prison, and then sent her draperies and carpets. "When winter came, many of the prisoners had no blankets and but little clothing. She gave them everything she had in her house that she could possibly spare and procured all she could from her neighbors. . . . She took up every carpet she had and cut it into pieces the size of a blanket in order to relieve the suffering of those poor prisoners."[12]

But it was through her books that Amanda made the greatest contribution. She reached more lonely, homesick men through them than through the little food, medicine, and bedding she could supply alone. Books provided entertainment and mental escape during the long sad hours, and this must have been nearly as important as food and warmth. The mind could be relieved and nourished and warmed, if not the body. Ovid Futch also discovered the importance to prisoners of something to read while researching his doctoral dissertation, a study of Andersonville based on soldiers' letters and diaries. He wrote: "Prison life would have been less dreary for many if reading material had been plentiful, but those who wished to read had little or no choice. Bibles and New Testaments seem to have outnumbered all other books combined within the stockade."[13] At Cahaba, in contrast, any prisoner who wished could have in his hands books on virtually any subject, and also knowledge that nearby, just outside the stockade, lived someone who cared.

Mrs. Gardner had a large and choice library left to her by an uncle who lived earlier at Cahaba but moved away. She had complete sets of the novels of Scott, Dickens, Bulwer-Lytton, and others. She had "all the standard poets in handsome binding." There were histories, biographies, books of travel, works on science, philosophy, and religion.[14] A prisoner had but to send a note by a guard to Amanda or Belle. The guard delivered the book and the same means was used to return it. The notes led Grigsby to his fantasy about Belle.

He was a farmer's son from Potosi, in Grant County, Wisconsin. He joined the Seventh Wisconsin Infantry and took part in Grant's Vicksburg campaign. He was captured by partisans while on a detail seeking a cache of cotton supposedly secreted in a Mississippi swamp. He arrived at Cahaba in April 1864. He was nineteen. "I noticed that many of the prisoners were reading books and pamphlets. Some of these books were new and nicely bound, others much worn and evidently the worse for prison use. By inquiring I found that these books were furnished to the prisoners by a young lady who lived near the prison."[15]

Other prisoners told Grigsby to send a note to a Miss

Belle if he wanted a book. His first effort brought a novel by Scott, which he read and returned. He received another, and thereafter "had something to read all the time, as did every other prisoner." He began sending notes of appreciation with his requests, making each a little longer and a bit less formal. Soon he was receiving messages from Belle in return with each book. "Young as I was, naturally fond of adventure and the natural bent of my mind stimulated by constant reading of Scott's, Bulwer's and other novels, is it any wonder that my correspondence with this young lady began to seem to me romantic and that I began to entertain for her feelings stronger than gratitude?"[16]

Grigsby developed a passionate desire to view his correspondent, and asked a guard to point out the Gardner home. The guard indicated a house across Capitol Street. Grigsby began volunteering to cook for men who did not like the chore so he could spend more time in the yard reserved for the many smoky cooking fires. A high board fence enclosed it. Grigsby enlarged a crack between the boards with a small knife. He watched the house suggested by the guard. For several days most of his time was spent with an eye at the hole as he waited for a look at the "damsel whom my excited imagination had pictured as possessing all the beauty, loveliness, grace, and other heroine qualities of a Rebecca." He sent a note by a guard asking Belle to appear at a certain hour on the porch of the house. He watched and waited day after day, but in vain. He gave up only when he was transferred to Andersonville, when the "materials for an exquisite romance in real life were rudely broken and scattered."[17]

Not until he returned to Alabama seeking Amanda and Belle did he discover that during all those days of squinting through the hole in the fence longing for a glimpse of the young lady who sent him notes, he watched the wrong house.[18]

Jesse Hawes also wrote of Mrs. Gardner, telling of her contributions of food, blankets, medicines, and the books from her library. "Those who met her always spoke of her as a bright, sunny Christian woman." He said "Little Belle" often passed gifts of vegetables into the prison. "Watching a time when a kind-hearted guard was stationed on the side of the stockade next to her yard, the little girl would bring her offerings to the hole in the stockade, the guard would call some prisoner and pass the gift to him, and one mess at least would be envied by the whole prison so long as the precious food was in sight or memory."[19]

Hawes said his squad never benefited from Mrs. Gardner's presents of food, "but we could not be blind to the humanity of one noble family." He ended his account of her by writing, "Dear noble, kind-hearted woman, her memory is cherished with feelings of reverence by the men who were grateful witnesses to her angelic deeds."[20]

Mrs. Gardner's gifts of food resulted in trouble with Lieutenant Colonel Jones. Hawes said an unfriendly guard saw Belle pass something through the stockade wall and reported the incident to Jones. After that, no more food came from the Gardners. She further aroused Jones's ire by protesting the punishment of prisoners on the ladder only a few feet from her home, punishment administered within view of the Gardner children who watched from their windows. Hawes claimed Jones told Mrs. Gardner, "Your sympathy for the damned Yankees is odious to me. Now bear yourself with the utmost care in the future or you shall be an exile." Grigsby said Captain Henderson interceded on Mrs. Gardner's behalf, "endorsing all she had done," and she was not troubled more by Jones.[21] However, the prisoners did not record whether the ladder was moved or whether the punishments on it continued.

Mrs. Gardner's youngest son, William, was called to duty late in the war and fought in the militia which helped defend Selma, taken by General James H. Wilson's cavalry on the same day that Grant captured Richmond. William, then seventeen, was returned unharmed to his mother by Union soldiers. Grigsby said this was because Wilson's men heard of her kindness to the prisoners and so rewarded her.[22]

Hawes said some of Wilson's troopers even asked permission to ride ahead of the main body to surround the Gardner home and protect her in the event of fighting or Confederate retaliation. Wilson, he said, granted the permission.[23]

Mrs. Gardner saved more than a hundred of the requests she received from the inmates of Castle Morgan but lost that many more when she moved to Selma. She also had letters and presents sent her after the war. Grigsby thought she deserved a greater reward and corresponded with members of the Congress seeking an act for her relief. He was told, however, that such a measure might result in thousands of similar requests, a precedent the Congress should not establish.[24]

After Grigsby's visit, Mrs. Gardner moved to New York City, and he lost further contact with her. While in Selma, however, he copied and preserved some of the notes she received from inside Castle Morgan. Michael O'Farrel of the 118th Illinois Mounted Infantry wrote, "Please excuse me from troubling you for a little vinegar, as I have a high fever every day and crave it, and I believe it would do me much good." J. R. Bowen, Charles Reynolds, Charles Harris, and James Farrell wrote simply, "Will you please send some books to the subscribers to while away the hours of prison life?" Private B. F. Daughtery, Company H, Thirty-seventh Regiment of Illinois Volunteers, wanted "some nice interesting book to read," and promised, "I will return it with care." Clement Ballinger asked to borrow a tub for him and four friends to wash their clothes.[25] C. W. Hayes,

Amanda and Belle 87

a hospital steward with the Third Illinois Volunteer Cavalry, wrote an emotional goodbye as the prison was being closed late in the war.

Kind Madam! We are all about to bid farewell to Castle Morgan. Some are already on their homeward journey. We will soon follow, rejoicing we are once more free. I feel I cannot leave without expressing my heartfelt thanks to you for the noble and humane kindness you have so generously bestowed on the prisoners while confined here. . . . Be assured, Kind Madam, that when we are once more surrounded by kind and loving friends, and in the enjoyment of all that makes life happy and agreeable, our thoughts will often revert to our kind benefactress at Cahaba. Many a silent prayer will be sent heavenward that you and your loving family may be spared the horrors of this unnatural and relentless war. Many a man will speak in glowing terms of that noble generosity and you will ever be remembered as a friend of the unfortunate. . . . May heaven's richest blessings descend upon you and your darling family.[26]

And there was this letter from Andrew McFarland on January 18, 1864:

Respected Madam: An unfortunate prisoner of war begs you will excuse the liberty he has taken in thus addressing you. Your many acts of kindness to us will ever be gratefully remembered. If possible to repay you, how gladly would we. But Madam, we know your noble heart would resent any such offer, and we have only the opportunity left us to return you the heartfelt thanks of all the prisoners. And now I trespass on your kindness still further. My time of service has nearly expired. I do most earnestly desire to be exchanged. If within your power, or by your kindly influence, to assist me, the remembrance of the happiness you would confer on an unfortunate man, I am sure, would repay your generous nature.[27]

Mrs. Gardner apparently took the plea to Captain Henderson, for Belle added at the end of McFarland's letter: "Note—My mother secured his exchange and he went his way rejoicing."[28]

7

The Muggers and
Big Tennessee

A contingent of thugs roamed among the thousands in Castle Morgan as in other prisons for captured Federal soldiers. They were called raiders and "N'Yaarkers" at Andersonville, and simply muggers at Cahaba. The difference in terms likely stemmed from New York City being little represented at Castle Morgan, since most of the men came from western states. In Andersonville, however, as William Best Hesseltine pointed out, "The majority of the 'raiders' were from New York City, and their fellow prisoners described them as the scourings of the city's slums." Whether in Cahaba or elsewhere, the thugs sought to improve their lot by preying on other prisoners, taking anything that could be converted to extra provisions, comforts, or privileges purchased from guards. They stole food, firewood, blankets, clothing, shoes, and money, and did not hesitate to include the sick and dying among their victims. Sometimes they attacked the helpless merely out of a perverted sense of fun, and nearly always they acted as a group, for it was in organization that they found strength. While hangings and beatings by their fellow prisoners finally curbed their depredations in Andersonville, one man is said to have accomplished the task in Cahaba.[1] According to Jesse Hawes, this man, nearly seven feet tall and armed only with huge fists, brought order where an inmate police force and court failed.

Hawes gave the man's name as George Pierce and said he was a member of the Third Tennessee Cavalry. A search of the surviving records fails to discover a George Pierce in the regiment, but there was a Richard M. Pierce of Company D, and it is possible that Hawes, writing from memory after twenty years, mistakenly recalled the name as George instead of Richard. Hawes's story of the man, also known as Big Tennessee, is supported by the account of another soldier intrigued by a seven-foot man from a Tennessee unit on board the *Sultana*.[2] Although no other Cahaba inmate told of the incidents involving Pierce as described by Hawes, there is no reason to doubt him, since there is independent confirmation of such a man, and Hawes gave the only detailed account of the prison. Here, too, Hawes was an eyewitness and was not relating secondhand reports.

Private Richard Pierce was not a Tennessean after all, but a blue-eyed, light-haired Kentucky farmer born at Barbourville, in Knox County. He volunteered on September 1, 1862, at Barbourville at the age of twenty-two, signing his enlistment papers with his mark, an X, over which his name was written by someone else. Colonel William C. Pickens, then commanding the Third Tennessee, signed as recruiting officer. Pierce, who served as a wagoner, was captured at Cumberland Gap, Tennessee, on March 26, 1863, and imprisoned at Richmond until paroled on June 13, at City Point, Virginia. He rejoined Company D at Nashville on August 31, 1863.[3]

The Third Tennessee originally was an East Tennessee outfit that recruited first at Cumberland Gap, where the

Virginia, Tennessee, and Kentucky borders meet, on August 10, 1862, under the authority of Governor Andrew Johnson. Pierce's hometown of Barbourville is only about twenty miles to the northwest. Other men joined at Murfreesboro, and the regiment entered U.S. service officially on January 27, 1863. It was sent to Nashville later that year where recruiting continued. The regiment's duties for several months largely involved escorting hospital and supply wagons in the Nashville area. It then became part of Brigadier General W. Sooy Smith's forces on his raid into Mississippi in February 1864. There the regiment met for the first time the man who would be its nemesis, the Confederate cavalry genius Nathan Bedford Forrest. He sharply repulsed Smith's forces and hotly pursued the fleeing Federals. At Ivey Farm, about ten miles from Okolona, Mississippi, Smith made a stand, and the Third Tennessee took part in a charge that checked Forrest and killed his brother, Colonel Jeffrey Forrest. Smith then resumed his retreat to the safety of Memphis. Soon thereafter the Third Tennessee returned to Nashville. It remained in that area until dispatched to Decatur, Alabama, under command of Lieutenant Colonel John B. Minnis in June. A battalion of the regiment fought at Big Name Creek, near Pond Springs, Alabama, on July 29, and another detachment saw action at Moulton on August 17. The regiment took part, too, in the fighting against Major General Joseph Wheeler during his raid into Tennessee in late August and early September.[4]

When General Sherman left Atlanta burning to begin his march to the sea in September 1864, General John B. Hood took his defeated Confederate army north in hopes of disrupting the Federal supply line and capturing Nashville. He sought thus to force Sherman to chase him and abandon Georgia. He sent Forrest's cavalry sweeping ahead to scout and to clear the way. Forrest crossed the Tennessee

River at Muscle Shoals and drove east to strike the railroad at Athens, Alabama, defended by a fort garrisoned with elements of the 106th, 110th, and 114th U.S. colored troops. At Forrest's approach, members of the Third Tennessee and infantry of the Eighteenth Michigan and the 102nd Ohio hurried north from Decatur, eighteen miles away, to assist the fort. They ran into heavy resistance while still a mile distant, but fought to within musket range only to receive grape, canister, and shell from the very fort they sought to relieve, which still flew the U.S. flag. They discovered too late that the place had been surrendered earlier without a fight and was occupied by Forrest's troops. The relief column of about four hundred men was surrounded and forced to surrender. Total Union losses that day, September 24, 1864, were 950, nearly all captured. Forrest lost 5 killed and 25 wounded. Among the captured Union men were 150 members of the Third Tennessee. Among them also was Sergeant H. C. Aldrich of Jerome, Michigan, who wrote about Cahaba, and Corporals A. Lewis Jennings and Edwin Ford, who wrote letters home to Hillsdale, Michigan.[5]

The following day, Forrest surrounded the remaining elements of the Third Tennessee at Sulphur Trestle on the Nashville and Decatur Railroad, and took 400 men prisoner at Blockhouses Number Seven and Eight, including Big Tennessee. Forrest therefore virtually eliminated the Third Tennessee in two days. But it may be said that he did it in a most humane fashion, since in all its fighting in Mississippi, Tennessee, and Alabama, the Third Tennessee suffered only 10 men killed or mortally wounded.[6]

Most of the white soldiers taken in the skirmishes at Athens and Sulphur Trestle were marched to Cahaba, and thus Big Tennessee, a prisoner of war for the second time, passed through the gates of Castle Morgan and on to his meeting with the muggers. The captured black soldiers were taken to Mobile and forced to labor on the defenses of the city.[7]

In good measure, the thieves and cutthroats in camps for prisoners of war were there because of the bounty system used to recruit soldiers for the North. Often a man could get more than $1,000 just for enlisting, a handsome sum in those days. Cities, counties, states, the Federal government, and even private organizations bought recruits to fill quotas, and paid most freely for them. By 1864 the contributions from Washington alone reached $300 per man, and that was besides what a man could claim from other sources. The sums became enormous. New York paid more than $86 million to buy recruits. In Illinois, Cook County, which includes Chicago, paid $2,801,239, and all Illinois counties together spent $13,711,389. Many an unsavory fellow jumped at the opportunity for the easy money such a system offered. He collected his bounty and as quickly as possible deserted to enlist again somewhere else for yet another bounty. In the jargon of the day it was called "leppin' the bounty," and was the means to a princely income. One man confessed to "leppin' " and collecting thirty-two times, and some received as much as $8,000 total for all their enlistments.[8] But inevitably some of them were sent into combat before an opportunity to desert arose, and some of these were captured and put into southern prison camps. The outright thugs among them formed gangs to prey on their fellow prisoners.

Harried and overworked prison officials and guards paid little attention to thievery and altercations among the prisoners, leaving to the inmates themselves the problems of internal order. At Andersonville, the much-beset prisoners formed a vigilance committee and hanged six of the "N'Yaarkers" with the blessings of Brigadier General Winder. Most of these were bounty-jumpers from New York who had infested the Belle Isle prison near Richmond be-

94 **The Muggers and Big Tennessee**

fore their transfer to Andersonville. Besides those hanged, eighteen men were forced to run a gauntlet and three of them died of their injuries.[9]

Such unsavory types in Castle Morgan were relatively few, "not a tithe of our whole body," according to Jesse Hawes. However, "they were for a time more than a match for all of us. They were organized, or at least quite well understood each other. The rest were not organized." They chose newcomers to the prison as their primary victims, since such men were most likely to have something of value. In one method of assault, two of the thugs would accost a new man, one throwing an arm about his neck and choking him while the other went through his pockets. The victim then was released "and with a blow sent stunned and staggering off into the darkness, or left temporarily senseless on the ground." Hawes claimed the Cahaba thieves obtained chloroform by bribing guards and anesthetized sleeping victims so they could be robbed without resistance. Credence is lent such a story by surgeon E. H. C. Bailey's report from the medical depot at Demopolis that he had on hand in October 1864 supplies that included thirty-four pounds of chloroform, indicating availability. An attempt to anesthetize a sergeant named Raymond of the Fourth Missouri Cavalry, led to the formation of a police committee and court such as that in Andersonville. Raymond struggled awake before the fumes could take effect and drove off his attacker. The following day he pointed the man out, and the mugger was seized by other prisoners. They chose a civilian, William Rea, as judge, and Andrew Conn, a tall, athletic member of the Third Kentucky Cavalry, as head of a police committee. The court sentenced Raymond's attacker, a man named Thompson, to be chained each night to a log.[10]

The court, however, did not last long. Rea, a wealthy farmer from Illinois captured by partisans while en route to visit his two sons in Sherman's army, was released. Conn left with the group transferred to the prison at Meridian. Additionally, several of the muggers infiltrated the police committee and rendered the system ineffective.[11] That finally did not matter, for Big Tennessee arrived.

Hawes described Big Tennessee as nearer to seven feet tall than to six, with large, muscular arms a foot longer than those of an ordinary man, and with chest and shoulders "enormous even for a man of his gigantic dimensions. . . . But with all his physical power, his manner was that of one of the mildest of men. Indeed, he seemed an overgrown boy, who would be too timid to defend his own rights, let alone the possibility of being the champion of the rights of others."[12]

That such a tall man, one who would have looked down upon Abraham Lincoln, was in the Union army was not altogether unusual. There were others. Captain Van Buskirk of the Twenty-seventh Indiana, for example, was only an inch and a half short of seven feet. However, the normal height was much less, and such men must have appeared as giants. *Harper's Weekly* carried an item on August 19, 1865, that said that figures kept by recruiters in twelve states during 1864 showed that the average height of enlistees was a trifle under 5 feet, 6½ inches, shorter than Big Tennessee by a foot and more.[13]

The time of the muggers in Castle Morgan ran out soon after the arrival of Private Pierce and his fellow cavalrymen from the fights at Athens and Sulphur Trestle. One of the first victims among the newcomers was a friend of the big man. On the following morning the young man searched the prison and located his assailants. He then went to his champion. Big Tennessee had the victim confront the muggers. While the youth talked with them, he approached as if a curious spectator. Four of the thugs surrounded the boy and threatened to beat him if he caused trouble. Big

Tennessee spoke up for his companion. The muggers then turned on the big man and threatened him also. One was behind, one to his right, and two in front. The discussion became more heated, and two of the men suddenly struck Big Tennessee. He shook off the blows and slapped his big left hand backward into the face of the man behind him. He then smashed his right fist into the face of the man on his right. Both the muggers collapsed. He grabbed the two astounded men in front by their hair and slammed their heads together, and then tossed them unconscious to the ground. No fight remained in any of the men when they roused themselves. "Sick, faint from the terrible shock each had received, they slowly arose and walked away, or were assisted to depart by their confederates."[14]

No one else offered to fight Big Tennessee in Castle Morgan. "Those who had seen the evidence of his prowess would as soon attack a catapult or an enraged elephant."[15] Word spread and other victims sought his aid. His presence alone was enough to decide any issue. A sick Ohio boy was robbed of his small supply of cooking wood, and Jesse Hawes reported the theft to Tennessee. The giant escorted the victim to the robber and ordered the wood returned. "Here, Ohio, pick up your wood and take it back," he told the boy, placing his hand on the shoulder of the thief. There was no resistance.

On another occasion, several men sought fun at the expense of a youth too sick to leave his bed on the ground. They decided on a cold overcast day that he was dirty and infested with lice and needed a bath. They stripped him and began to roughly scrub him with sand and water. Big Tennessee intervened and said quietly to the sick young man, "Boy, put on your clothes and go back to your bed if you want to." The tormentors did not protest. Hawes said the young victim died during the following night.[16]

Within a few weeks, Hawes wrote, most of the muggers

volunteered to join the Confederate army. He said he believed part of their reason was to get away from Big Tennessee. They were let out of the prison and out of his intimidating presence.

Hawes closed his account of Big Tennessee by saying he probably died in the *Sultana* disaster. However, William A. McFarland of the Forty-second Indiana Infantry, remembered a survivor of the wreck who was an unusually tall man from a Tennessee unit. He attracted McFarland's notice after the boat stopped at Memphis, the day before it exploded, and some of the men went into the city. Big Tennessee got drunk in Memphis, and an armed guard was required to return him to the *Sultana*. "He was a thin seven-footer, and he came down to the boat shouting and cursing, at the point of bayonets, so drunk he could hardly walk. He was brought up to the hurricane deck, where he caused considerable disturbance."[17]

McFarland, who was an Andersonville inmate and therefore could not have known of Big Tennessee before boarding the *Sultana,* saw him in the water shortly after the boat exploded, and again at dawn hours later and about seven miles farther downstream. McFarland had been picked up by a yawl sent out by the steamboat *Silver Spray,* and the next person the yawl approached was the big man. He sat on a log. "He asked how far it was to Memphis, and when told only a mile, he said to the crew, 'Go to hell with your boat; if you couldn't come to help me before now you had better have stayed away.' "[18]

With that, the man slid off his log and began stroking the swollen and muddy Mississippi toward Memphis. He was on the dock before the *Silver Spray* arrived, apparently still intoxicated and resisting being taken to a hospital. Several soldiers were knocked down, McFarland said, before an armed guard was detailed to march him through the streets to medical attention. The man created further disturbance by grabbing clothing from merchants' store-front stalls as he passed, and knocking down several merchants as well.[19]

To deny that this man was Big Tennessee would suppose that there was another such soldier from a Tennessee regiment in Castle Morgan who also was aboard the *Sultana*. That is most unlikely. What of the difference in descriptions from Jesse Hawes's heavily muscled gladiator to McFarland's thin seven-footer? Six months in Cahaba Federal Prison on a diet mainly of ground corn would account for that. As for the change in disposition from mild-mannered in the early days of his confinement to the raging lout aboard the *Sultana* and at Memphis, one need only to again consider the ravages and trauma of those six months in prison and add the effects of too much unaccustomed liquor on a half-starved body. The available evidence shows that Hawes and McFarland did write of the same man.

Private Richard Pierce was reported at first as among those killed in the disaster on the Mississippi. A casualty sheet is in his records which says he "Perished by the explosion of the Steamer 'Sultana.' " A later document, however, shows the section about his death lined out and the information added that he reported for duty on May 3. The Memphis *Daily Bulletin* of April 28 listed him as among the survivors treated at the Gayoso Hospital, although it spelled his name Pearce rather than Pierce. The May 3 reporting date in his records indicates a six-day stay in the Gayoso, where 138 of the victims were treated. He was given transportation from Memphis to Nashville and there mustered out on May 17 with an effective date of June 10, then passing forever from history's further notice.[20]

8
Mutiny, Flood, Freedom

The last four months in the brief history of Castle Morgan were extraordinary. The steamboat load of clothing and other supplies for the prisoners arrived in December 1864 but, of course, did not last long. New clothes, shoes, and blankets will not satisfy hungry men who desperately need something to quiet the awful and incessant pleading of empty bellies. They bartered away the fresh bounty to their guards for food. Afterward, they were hungry again and as ill-clothed and equipped as before, but now unprepared in deepening winter. Very cold weather came late in January and it even snowed, rare so far south. Men sought warmth on bitter mornings by forming groups and running in circles until too tired to continue.[1] A few of the prisoners staged an uprising just before the severe weather, but none got away. For two or three days afterward, until Captain Henderson and Lieutenant Colonel Jones identified the leader of the trouble, the men went hungry and shivered without fires. They got nothing, not even their usual skimpy cornmeal and occasional bit of bad meat. If endless hunger and the damp cold were insufficient plagues, the rivers rose at the coming of March and flooded both town and prison with several feet of dirty, chocolate-colored water. No dry place remained to the Union men but in the warehouse rafters or the higher bunks under the leaky roof, and these accommodated few. No fires were possible for warming and drying the body or cooking food except two or three built on rafts, debris, or atop the prison wall.

The occasional accidental dunking of a prisoner or a Rebel enlivened those miserable days, and one prisoner said the flood brought definite benefit. "It drowned the rats out of their holes in the walls so that we got a few to eat, and it drowned out the graybacks," wrote Sergeant Aldrich.[2] The "graybacks" in this instance, of course, were lice.

None of it mattered very much finally, for the end of the war approached. After those most dismal days the men were freed at last and finally could lift their heads and show their backs to Castle Morgan and Bell Tavern. They could go home. Despite their suffering, most left in better shape—according to their own army—than some later wanted to admit. They left their dead, too, of course, and left those too sick or hurt to travel, and more graves were to be dug in the little cemetery west of town.

Sadly for the townspeople, the flood drowned their final remaining hope for Cahaba and could be seen as symbolic of the last futile struggles of the South, the Confederacy's death throes being much advanced even as the rivers washed away Cahaba's future.

The uprising by the prisoners caused the most excitement before the flood and the final exodus. It was the work of Captain Hiram S. Hanchett of Company M, Sixteenth Illinois Cavalry. Cavalrymen of General Nathan Bedford Forrest, who seemed determined always to keep Castle Morgan filled, captured him near Nashville on December

The unfortunate Captain Hiram Hanchett, probably murdered by Lieutenant Colonel Jones, as depicted by Jesse Hawes (Jesse Hawes, *Cahaba: A Story of Captive Boys in Blue*)

3, 1864. He made an appalling mistake when he saw he was about to be taken, surreptitiously removing his uniform and donning civilian clothing in the belief that civilians quickly were freed. A fine officer he might have been, but he thought none too clearly that day. The moment he changed clothes, he became subject to a charge of spying and open to a spy's punishment. He further incriminated himself by shaving his beard and moustache, and giving his name as George Schellar. The provost marshal of the Army of Tennessee registered him by that name and sent him southward to Cahaba.[3]

Hanchett, thirty-nine, was a lawyer from Woodstock, Illinois. Jesse Hawes described him as 5 feet, 7½ inches, with thin dark hair and dark "searching and intelligent" eyes. The captain's reason for planning what all Confederate records call a mutiny is obvious. As Hawes said: "The legal education of Captain Hanchett made him fully aware that the repudiation of his military rank and the pretense of being a citizen was a violation of the most firmly settled rules of war, and the fact of discovery would almost certainly lead his captors to inflict some form of punishment."[4]

Such awareness, however, did not require a legal education. Almost any soldier in blue or gray knew the penalty for pretending to be a civilian. The longer Hanchett remained in Castle Morgan, the greater the threat of discovery and execution as a spy. He had to get out. He must have learned soon that many had tried, few or none successfully. Even if he got beyond the town limits, he would be alone deep in hostile territory. He needed help and only his fellow prisoners could provide it.

Captain Hanchett evolved a most intricate plan during the few weeks he spent inside Castle Morgan. Hawes wrote about it at length. The Union men would overpower the entire guard force. Armed with the guards' weapons, they would march on Selma and capture its arsenal. Then, all armed, they would separate into small groups and make their way south to Union-held Pensacola on the Gulf. A selected group could gallop ahead on captured horses and arouse the Pensacola garrison to march out and rescue the approaching Federals. If the escapees found a steamboat at Selma, it could carry the advance force down the Alabama for nearly the whole distance. Most of Alabama's Confederate troops were in the northern half of the state, and no force available in the region could stop the men of Castle Morgan once they took Selma. There might be casualties but Captain Hanchett easily could justify his actions. As Hawes said, "If lives were sacrificed in the undertaking, the loss might not exceed the deaths that would result from remaining confined at Castle Morgan."[5]

The scheme was that of a desperate man ignoring reality. Captain Hanchett simply was not the soldier Colonel Chandler warned in his inspection report might take command of the prisoners and lead an unstoppable rebellion.[6] The plan depended on unarmed men overpowering an armed guard in the prison and then the entire garrison and town, traveling ten miles, and capturing a larger city. They then would be about 125 airline miles from Pensacola and much farther by the river or the muddy roads. Any cross-country route presented many creeks, swamps, and thick woods. Men well organized and in the best condition might accomplish a like mission deep in enemy territory, but Hanchett had no such troops. He had hungry, ill-clad men from many different units who had never trained together. In addition, he informed only a few prisoners in fear that his plans might leak to the guards, and most of the men knew him only as a civilian. Yet he expected the whole prison population to rise at his command.

Hanchett's scheme for capturing the guards in the prison was a bit more realistic, but not much. At night, when the

Rebels locked the prisoners inside the warehouse, nine guards patrolled just outside, within the stockade. At guard change both the incoming and outgoing squads, along with a corporal, were in the cook yard together for a few moments. The Confederates usually built a large fire to provide light and heat. Hanchett's men then would beg permission to leave the warehouse and warm themselves at the fire. During the last guard change before daylight, they would overpower the nineteen guards silently with the help of men from the warehouse. Dressed in the guards' clothing and armed with their weapons, the Union men could sneak out of the prison and capture the remaining Confederate troops, who, Hanchett hoped, would lie helplessly asleep in their quarters.[7]

The uprising failed form the first moment. The gate was just being opened when Hanchett's men struck at 3 A.M. They struck too soon. Although they overpowered the nine guards already inside, the corporal entering with the relief force heard the scuffling and cries, and immediately backed out. He slammed and barred the gate and gave the alarm. Hoping yet to succeed with a quick charge on the gate, Hanchett shouted into the warehouse, according to Hawes, "I want a hundred men, men of courage, to fall in immediately!" Some said he shouted more simply, "Give me a hundred men!" He got none. Most of the prisoners did not know of the plan and the cause of the disturbance. In a few moments, the stockade gate was reopened to present the prisoners with the specter of a nine-pounder cannon pointed at them and all guards mobilized for combat. Lieutenant Colonel Jones demanded immediate release of the captured Rebels, who were locked in the water closet. He threatened to blow the prisoners "from hell to breakfast" with his cannon. John Walker remembered a brave—or reckless—Yankee who yelled back at Jones, "Is she cocked and primed? Let her go!" After more threats, the prisoners freed the captured guards and Jones began a search for the Union leaders. None gave away Hanchett. Jones was further stymied because the captured guards could identify none of their attackers.[8]

Henderson and Jones told the prisoners they would have no food or fires until they produced their leaders. Some claimed they spent three of the cold January days with nothing to eat before Hanchett surrendered rather than see the men suffer more. Daniel Garber of Company E, 102nd Ohio Volunteer Infantry, remembered it as forty-eight hours. While they waited hungry and shivering, Jones forced the men to pass naked between two files of Rebels, holding their clothing above their heads, because a guard had told Jones he wounded one of the men with a bayonet during the uprising. Jones found no injured Federal, however. "The man was wounded in the hand, so they didn't get him," recalled Perry Summerville. Walker said the wound was in the wrist and the man covered it in the clothes bundle he held overhead.[9]

Captain Henderson filed a report on the incident on January 23, informing Brigadier General J. D. Imboden, then in charge of military prisons west of the Savannah River, that, "On the morning of Friday, January 20, there was a mutiny in the Federal prison under my command. . . . During the excitement, not a single prisoner effected his escape." He said investigation showed that George Schellar, "alias Captain Hanchett," led the uprising. He had ordered the man, "a most unmitigated scoundrel," secured with irons and confined with seven of his companions in the county jail's dungeon, Henderson said.

"The most probable conjecture is that he dressed himself as a citizen and put himself in position to be captured, for the purpose of obtaining information of the strength and movements of the Confederate forces. . . . He is an exceedingly dangerous and bad man."[10]

Lieutenant Colonel Jones added his endorsement to Captain Henderson's report: "Respectfully forwarded for the information of and orders from the brigadier general commanding the prison department. I am fully convinced that Captain Hanchett, alias Schellar, is a spy and a dangerous man and deserves a spy's fate."[11]

Imboden considered the evidence from Cahaba and instructed Henderson and Jones to return all those under arrest to the prison except Hanchett. He informed the secretary of war on February 15 that "I have ordered a trial on the charge of being a spy, the result of which will be communicated to the War Department as soon as ascertained." He simultaneously issued a general order that said the guard at all the prisons under his authority should immediately fire on all future mutineers, and upon the whole body of prisoners if necessary. "And every prisoner found with arms in his hands at the time of any mutiny or forcible attempt to escape shall be instantly shot to death; and this penalty will in no case be remitted where such armed prisoner is overpowered by or surrendered to the guard on the suppression of a mutiny."[12]

Imboden had the warning, which meant death to any rebelling prisoner found with arms even if he surrendered without resistance, circulated in all prisons under his command. "Their own conduct will then determine whether their lives are to be spared or not," he said. It seems out of place that in such a brutal order he also spoke of "that humanity becoming the Christian people of these Confederate States," who "have not yet learned to forget their own high civilization."[13]

Union Major General George H. Thomas, commander of the Army of the Cumberland, sent a stern warning of his own on April 4. Addressing it to Lieutenant General Taylor, whose command included Alabama, he said he learned from a letter that Hanchett faced trial. He denied

Hanchett entered Confederate lines except as an officer with troops, and warned, "Should he be convicted and punished as a spy I assure you I shall make most ample retaliation."[14] However, General Thomas' support and threats could not help Captain Hanchett by then. He already was dead.

Captain Henderson and Lieutenant Colonel Jones did not convene a court to try Captain Hanchett. Henderson left Cahaba for a new assignment, and the flood and the approaching end of the war intervened. Hanchett remained locked in the small dungeon in the county jail under the care of jailer G. G. Ogletree until release of the other prisoners. He was freed either on April 2 or the next day—the record is unclear—and invited to breakfast by J. A. Haweth, a member of the town council. While they sat at Haweth's table, a Lieutenant Robinson, who was Jones's adjutant, arrived with two soldiers of the guard, P. B. Vaughn and Phelin Vaughn, Jr. They said they were under orders to take Hanchett to Demopolis for exchange and freedom. The unsuspecting captain gladly left with them and disappeared forever.[15] Investigators later could not find his body or determine his fate, but charged Lieutenant Colonel Jones with his murder. He is remembered in the little cemetery at Cahaba where small monuments lie over empty graves. The one for him says, "In memory of Hiram S. Hanchett, Capt. Co. H., 16 Regt. Ill. Cav. Civil War. Apr. 3, 1865." Even that did not work out quite right for Captain Hanchett. The stone has him in the wrong unit. He belonged to Company M, not H.

The flood began during the afternoon of March 1, the Cahaba and Alabama rivers overflowing as they had so often before at Cahaba. The water rose slowly at first, seeping through the timber walls of the stockade. By midnight it covered the entire prison to a depth of several feet. C. M. Nisley, a native of Harrisburg, Pennsylvania, who enlisted at LaFayette, Indiana, in Company D, Fortieth Indiana Infantry, said it ranged from eighteen inches to three feet. Jesse Hawes said it was knee-deep. John Walker remembered it as up to four feet. Most of the men stood in the water nightlong. Some climbed into the upper bunks, called "roosts" by the men, but the bunks were not safe for too many at a time. Hawes said a large number crowded onto one "and their weight crushed it to the earth, or, rather, water."[16]

The following morning Hawes and several sergeants among the prisoners waded into the outer yard and asked an officer for an audience with Lieutenant Colonel Jones. Soon a boat arrived at the stairs leading to the elevated walkway around the top of the stockade. Jones climbed the stairs. Hawes saluted him and asked permission for the prisoners to move to higher ground nearby. Jones replied that he would not grant the prisoners so convenient an opportunity to escape. Hawes wrote: "The possibility of an escape at that time was an absurdity. The whole country was flooded. The whole prison was without shoes to their feet or covering to their backs. If they had been turned loose with permission to walk unmolested to their own armies, there were not twenty men in the whole three thousand who possessed enough endurance to have accomplished the feat."[17]

Sergeant Aldrich said the plight of the prisoners even touched some of the guards, who circulated a petition asking Jones to let the Union men move to the higher area. More than sixty signed it. Jones replied to his men that the prisoners would remain in the stockade until time for their burial. Walker recalled Jones's words as, "No! Not if every damned Yankee drowns."[18]

For three days and nights the men remained in the water, existing on the crackers the guards issued once a day. After that, Jones permitted a few at a time to go out and gather logs, roots, and other material with which to build islands in the water. Hawes recalled, "In a short time the inner prison was covered with little wood platforms, and the night found us high and dry." John Walker said his squad obtained a few pieces of heavy timber and cord wood "and for two days and two nights eight of us sat back to back on that wood."[19]

Many of the men became ill with diarrhea after a day or two in the flood and, with the water closet also awash, the result floated in the water trapped within the prison. Hawes called it "more nearly related to the contents of a city's sewer than the pearly drops that fall from heaven." Perry Summerville said it was so filthy "that we would wade out to the stockade and hold our cups to catch the clean water as it came through the cracks."[20]

A few humorous moments relieved the misery, at least dunkings in the highly polluted water were humorous to some, if not the victims. Hawes recalled a Tennessee man who stretched out atop the narrow warehouse wall. "For an hour or two he was motionless, then comfort required a change in his position; half-asleep, not remembering his novel location, he threw himself impatiently upon his side, and shot downward into the watery bed below." The man was unhurt, but as he spat the dirty water from his mouth he remarked he would "not go to sleep in that place again." A Confederate officer pranced his horse into Castle Morgan for a look at the Federals. He forgot the location of the sunken barrels used as a reservoir for the prison's drinking water, which were hidden by the flood. In a moment "horse and rider were down, floundering in the deep water" in front of hundreds of laughing men.[21]

Such incidents may be the reason at least one passerby thought the prisoners enjoyed themselves. Kate Cumming, a nurse with the Confederate Army of Tennessee, was aboard the steamboat *Southern Republic* as it struggled toward Montgomery against the swollen current. She said Cahaba stood in water four or five feet deep and people sailed about the town in boats. The spirit of the prisoners, she said, "if we were to judge by their actions and the noise they made, had not been dampened by prison life. They seemed rather pleased than otherwise with their chances for aquatic sports."[22]

Captain Henderson missed the flood, leaving Jones alone in charge of Cahaba during the prisoners' worst time. He left for a new assignment right after Captain Hanchett's mutiny, and a communication from General Winder on February 2 referred to him as "late commanding the prison at Cahaba." The message concerned seven hundred dollars in U.S. greenbacks belonging to prisoners. Henderson wanted to return it but said he had advanced them his own Confederate money, which they probably used to buy extra food, against the federal currency. Winder told him the quartermaster general bought U.S. dollars at five for one. He should exchange the money and then repay himself the sum he advanced, returning the balance to the prisoners.[23]

For some time much had been occurring that promised well for the prisoners. Their exchange and freedom neared and Henderson was an active participant in working out the details. For this reason, the Confederacy promoted him to lieutenant colonel and sent him to Vicksburg. With the South near collapse and pressure in the North growing to save the men dying in ill-supplied southern prison camps, General Grant relented on prisoner exchanges. He informed Secretary of War Stanton on January 21 that he authorized a resumption of negotiations on the matter and that Federal supplies were being sent through the lines to sustain Union men held by the Confederacy.[24]

Henderson began negotiations at Vicksburg for another steamboat load of material for the men in Cahaba pending their exchange. His Federal counterpart was Colonel A. C. Fisk. Recalled Henderson:

> Fisk casually remarked, "Why not bring the men here, under parole, and detain them in a camp on neutral ground until exchanged?" I caught up the suggestion, and added that I was ready to enter into such an arrangement if it were made to apply to the grays as well as to the blues.
>
> He agreed and before we parted drew up a cartel and the minor particulars in duplicate to be furnished the confirming authorities. The two governments ratified, and we set up the camp at Four-Mile Bridge, back of Vicksburg.[25]

The key points of the agreement, reached on February 21, were that the men of both sides would be kept on neutral ground and enjoy the benefit of Union food and material until the red tape of exchange could be unraveled. They would be under joint guard of Confederate and Union troops with each side able to see after its own. Further details were settled and added on March 16, 1865. This document was signed by Union Brigadier General Morgan L. Smith, commander of the District of Vicksburg, and Confederate Colonel N. G. Watts, the exchange agent for whom Henderson worked. It declared the neutral ground to be one mile and a half in width on either side of the railroad between Big Black bridge and Four-Mile bridge. Within that territory "no hostile person or persons belonging to the Federal or to the Confederate armies shall in anywise molest or interfere with the prisoners, officers or men, or transportation of either Government." The Union agreed to rebuild the railroad through the area and to construct a pontoon bridge over Big Black River across which Union and southern prisoners would walk in two-way traffic to freedom. Confederate troops would guard the Union end of the bridge on the west bank, Union troops the Confederate end on the east bank. General Smith and Colonel Watts at first named the neutral ground Aubrey Territory, but Lieutenant Colonel Henderson wanted it called Camp Fisk after Colonel Fisk, who suggested the plan, and so it was.[26]

The flood still swamped Castle Morgan when many of the prisoners began their departure from that unhappy place. Lieutenant Colonel Jones, despite his harsh comments about the Yankees drowning before they left Colonel Hill's warehouse, sent about 700 to Selma at the height of the flood.[27] That left, however, about 2,300 still stranded, and conditions did not return to normal for ten days. Lieutenant Colonel Jones finally informed the prisoners they were being freed, and steamboats began arriving to take the men away. He called large groups out and paroled them on their oath not to take up arms against the South until officially exchanged. Remembered Hawes: "This performance over, the command, 'Right face' was given, and we were marched down to the landing and put on board an old steamboat, which soon after pushed out and started up stream, to the great delight of all the prisoners on board."[28]

Some of the men were carried by steamboat to Selma where they boarded the Alabama and Mississippi Rivers Railroad for the trip west. Other steamboats went downstream, taking the men south to where the boats could enter the Tombigbee River, just above Mobile Bay, and carry them up to the Demopolis and McDowell's Bluff area. From there they went to Meridian, Jackson, and then to Vicksburg and Camp Fisk.[29]

George Robinson, that persistent escapee who served three hitches in the Union army, left Cahaba on one of the steamboats that took the long river route. He recalled that it had four large cannon on the bow, and none worked after the prisoners finished. "Before we reached our des-

Mutiny, Flood, Freedom 113

Lieutenant Colonel H. A. M. Henderson, seated, at Camp Fisk, near Vicksburg, at the end of the war. Henderson helped negotiate establishment of Camp Fisk as neutral ground where Federal prisoners might await exchange. They were under Confederate control but able to receive Federal supplies. (Library of Congress)

114 **Mutiny, Flood, Freedom**

tination the boys had all four guns spiked with old files they found on the boat."[30]

The releases continued for more than a month. Sergeant Aldrich, for example, left on April 12, nearly four weeks after the departure of those in the Bell Tavern hospital who were well enough to travel. Men continued to improve and leave the hospital all through April. For some, however, the resumption of exchanges came just too late. The surgeons recorded the deaths of twenty-one prisoners in March and eight in April.[31]

Men from Cahaba were not the only ones sent to neutral Camp Fisk for the trip home. Prisoners also went from Andersonville, Macon, and other camps. As at Cahaba, death intervened. Desperately sick men collapsed on the roads leading to freedom and home. A most distressed Colonel Watts telegraphed Lieutenant General Taylor from Jackson on March 27, "Humanity, simply [sic] humanity, caused me to commit this breach of etiquette." He said hospitals at Jackson were too ill-equipped to help sick Union prisoners en route to Vicksburg. "They were dying on the roadside with no food and no one to feed them." The Federals offered to send ambulances and wagons under Confederate guard, and he agreed without clearing it with Taylor. "They sent their chief surgeon with me, under parole of honor to see nothing and say nothing." Unless the general objected, the Federal ambulances and wagons would continue to travel on those mercy missions within Confederate lines, "not only for their prisoners but ours," as long as necessary. He told Taylor he hoped feelings of humanity "will prompt you to forgive."[32] Taylor hardly could do otherwise.

On Good Friday, April 14, Union Major General Napoleon J. T. Dana, commander of the Department of Mississippi with headquarters at Vicksburg, wired Washington that the Confederacy had sent 4,700 Federal men to Camp

Fisk. He complained that General Wilson's raid through Alabama came at the wrong time for many prisoners. "The Confederates would have delivered here about 11,000 men if their communications had not been interrupted by Wilson." Of the men received, he said, 1,100 were sick, nearly all from Andersonville. "The rest of the prisoners are in excellent health, the Cahaba prisoners particularly."[33]

The afternoon of that same April 14, the *Sultana* tied up at the wharf at Cairo, Illinois, ending the first day of its trip down the Mississippi to New Orleans.[34] That night, John Wilkes Booth shot Abraham Lincoln.

9
The *Sultana*

The great white steamboat backed slowly from the landing at Memphis and, paddle wheels churning, eased forward to cross the Mississippi River in the darkness to the coal yard at Hopefield Point on the Arkansas shore. In an hour, a thousand bushels of fuel had been loaded aboard in burlap bags. Some of the blue-clad passengers helped. They had been too long from home and were eager to be going. Then the big packet nosed northward, bound for Cairo, Illinois, struggling under a great load, pushing against a swollen and strong current. The night was black except for twinkling lights aboard and those of Memphis fading astern. It was cloudy and a light rain fell.[1] The splashing of the great paddle wheels spanking the water on each side was joined by the creak and groan of overburdened timbers and planks, and joined also by the buzzing murmur of too many voices. The *Sultana*, the pride of Captain J. Cass Mason, usually danced through the water at up to twelve miles each hour. Now she moved heavily and her timbers creaked despite the sure hand of pilot George Clayton. It was about one o'clock in the morning of April 27, 1865.

117

The *Sultana* loaded with men newly released from Confederate prisons, most of them from Cahaba. The picture was taken at Helena, Arkansas, two days before the steamboat exploded near Memphis, killing most of those on board. (Library of Congress)

If Cass Mason frowned that morning in his "texas" cabin atop the boat, he had cause. He must have been one of the most worried men along the whole length of the Mississippi. He had been on the rivers too long for it to have been otherwise. He showed his concern when he told one of his officers as the *Sultana* left Memphis, "I'd give all the interest I have in this steamer if we were safely landed at Cairo." The *Sultana* likely was more overloaded than any vessel in Mississippi River and steamboat history. Probably 2,300 persons were aboard, nearly all newly released prisoners of war from Cahaba and Andersonville, with those from Cahaba being the majority. No one will ever know the exact number. Those making the passenger list became confused at the human flood pouring aboard at Vicksburg and missed identifying and counting many. Whatever the load, it was an impossible one for a packet rated for no more than 376 passengers and crew. Horses, mules, and hogs were aboard as well. Already, back at Helena, Arkansas, the last stop before Memphis, the boat almost overturned when a photographer set up his camera and hundreds and hundreds of men surged to the landward side in hopes of being in the photograph. The *Sultana* had taken on a frightening twenty-degree list and might have rolled on over had not Cass Mason and his crew quickly restored order with much shouting.[2]

The big boat began the trip carrying a shocking message southward. She had dropped down from St. Louis and arrived at Cairo shortly before word of Lincoln's assassination. Secretary of War Edwin M. Stanton, fearful of Rebel plots and seeing conspirators everywhere, ordered the news suppressed in all the military districts of the South. That included a vast stretch of the Mississippi, and the telegraph was silenced. Stanton, however, could not silence the passengers or keep them and the crew from carrying newspapers. The *Sultana* was the first boat to leave for the South and spread news of the president's murder all the way to New Orleans. The April 19 edition of the New Orleans *Picayune* gave credit. "By the arrival of the steamer *Sultana* we have received dates of the fifteenth: Official! President Lincoln was assassinated last night at Ford's Theater."[3]

New Orleans may have stopped a moment to catch its breath, but business continued, and the same issue of the *Picayune* carried an advertisement that the "large and commodious passenger steamer *Sultana*" would leave the following day and had "fine staterooms and everything that is calculated to make the trip a pleasant one."[4]

Cass Mason didn't leave on time, staying over in hopes

of increasing his northbound freight and the number of passengers. Business remained light, however, and the *Sultana* headed upriver a day late with seventy-six cabin passengers, a hundred hogsheads of sugar, a hundred hogs, and sixty horses and mules.[5]

Things began to go wrong almost immediately. The Mississippi was flooding, and the great downward rush of water would have to be battled the whole way. The melting snow and spring rains from much of the vast land between the eastern mountains and the Rockies funneled into the Mississippi in a surging tide of water, mud, trees, and whatever else the mighty river could gather up, a tide that began reaching New Orleans at the same time the *Sultana* began splashing the water northward. In addition to the problem of the flood, one of the *Sultana*'s boilers began leaking. It would have to be repaired. There would be further delay.

At Vicksburg, the thousands of men just released from Confederate prison camps at Cahaba and Andersonville awaited a boat ride up the river toward home. Some were emaciated, some maimed or crippled and still suffering the pain of wounds. Many were sick. All had endured southern prison camps where too many men had too little food and shelter and there was too much disease and death. Now they were in another crowded camp and they wanted to go home.

The *Sultana* was built for Captain Preston Lodwick at the John Litherbury yard in Cincinnati. The company of Moore and Richardson provided the machinery. She was completed in January, 1863, at a cost of sixty thousand dollars. When she departed her birthplace on February 4 bound for Pittsburgh with her first cargo, the Cincinnati *Daily Commercial* hailed her as "one of the largest and best business steamers ever constructed."[6]

She was registered at 660 tons and rated at 1,000 tons

capacity. Yet she drew just 34 inches of water. She measured 260 feet from bow to stern, had a beam of 42 feet, a deck width of 39 feet and a hold 7 feet deep. She was powered by four high-pressure boilers arranged horizontally side-by-side, each 18 feet long and 46 inches in diameter. Her two engines had cylinders 25 inches in diameter with 8-foot strokes. They drove side wheels measuring 34 feet in diameter that worked 11-foot buckets.[7]

Her main deck was for power plant, deck passengers, and freight. Livestock was confined in an area toward the stern. The boilers and engines were in a partitioned area near the middle of this deck. The second deck, misnamed the boiler deck, was reached by a wide stairway near the front of the superstructure. Running the length of its middle was the saloon, richly decorated, ornate, strung with glittering chandeliers. All along both walls of this social hall for the monied passengers were their cabins. A fifty-foot section aft was set aside as cabins for the ladies. A well-stocked bar was at the forward wall, surrounded by a semicircle of tables for bar customers. The next level was the hurricane deck, also called the promenade deck and also for deck passengers. Rising from the middle of this level was the texas, where the boat's officers lived at the very summit of the packet. Captain Mason's cabin occupied the forward end. Several stories are told about how the texas deck was named. One claims that another boat years before had rooms named after the states, having exactly enough rooms, and the nation having exactly enough states, to make an even match. Then Texas was admitted to the Union, making one state too many for the boat. Its officers responded, the story goes, by naming the cabin housing their quarters after the new state, and the usage spread until texas became the name for the officers' deck on all steamboats.[8]

Atop the forward end of the texas was the pilothouse where ruled the masters of steamboats when they were underway. The captain might be king on an ocean vessel, but on American rivers filled with tricky currents, snags, ever-shifting sandbars, and the debris of wrecks, the wise and experienced pilot, who knew the river and her ways, handled navigation. The pilot manned an immense wheel, always standing at one side of it, and aimed his boat with the aid of the tall jackstaff rising straight up from the bow. Bell and whistle pulls hung within easy reach and speaking tubes led downward for communicating with the engineer.

Being launched into the full bustle and uproar of the Civil War's midpoint, the *Sultana* did a brisk business, frequently serving as Union troop and supply ship. Business was so good that first year that the great white boat returned her owner more than twice her cost, and Lodwick decided to retire with his profits. He sold her to Cass Mason and five associates for a reported eighty thousand dollars. Mason owned one-sixteenth and the *Sultana*'s clerk, W. J. Gamboel, one-eighth.[9]

Mason had climbed rapidly in steamboating. No doubt he worked hard, but a wise marriage helped. He was a native of Lynchburg, Virginia, carried to the banks of the Missouri while still a child. He spent his working life on boats, serving as a clerk on several. He married Rowena Dozier in 1860, becoming the son-in-law of Captain James Dozier, owner of several fine packets. One of them was the *Rowena*.[10] It was fitting that the husband of the young woman become captain of the boat named for her, and Cass Mason secured his first command. It was not to be either a long or a happy business association. On February 13, 1863, the U.S. gunboat *New Era* stopped the *Rowena* near Island No. 10 for examination of her papers and cargo. On board were found two hundred ounces of quinine bound for Tiptonville, Tennessee, then still under Confederate control. Searchers also found nearly three thousand pairs of Confederate uniform pants. Ensign William C. Hanford, acting in command of the *New Era*, seized steamboat and cargo, and the *Rowena* became an addition to the U.S. Navy's river fleet. Mason was not arrested. Perhaps loss of his boat was deemed sufficient punishment, or he was not held responsible for the contraband. The navy and the government might be forgiving, but Mason's father-in-law apparently could not forgive loss of the boat, and all business association between the two ended. Nor did Dozier retrieve the *Rowena*. While still in navy service, she struck a snag at Devil's Island above Cape Giradeau, Missouri, and sank on April 18, 1863. Just three days before, Secretary of the Navy Gideon Welles had ordered her returned to Dozier provided she was not deemed indispensable to the war effort.[11]

Cass Mason was not a man easily defeated, and soon took a new command, the *Belle Memphis*, owned by the St. Louis and Memphis Packet Company, and in the St. Louis–New Orleans trade.[12] He left her when he bought an interest in the *Sultana* and became her captain.

After departing New Orleans on the morning of Friday, April 21, 1865, the *Sultana* plowed north, struggling against the great spring flood rushing down toward salt water. She called at Baton Rouge and Natchez, and at other way points. Friday and Saturday passed, and she was making slow time toward Vicksburg when Nathan Wintringer, the chief engineer, informed Captain Mason that one of the boilers was leaking. This was annoying, but not unusual. The boilers caused continual trouble. The boat had been forced to stop at Natchez for their repair on the previous trip, and at Vicksburg on the trip before that.[13]

The boilers on all steamboats were a problem, the main source of danger, and had been since the first steamboat, the *New Orleans*, went puffing and churning down the river in 1811 and 1812. A Negro on the Natchez bluffs is said to have tossed his hat and hooted, "Ole Mississippi done got her master now."[14] Well, she had not, being too wild and powerful for mastering before the arrival of more efficient technology. If the boilers that drove boats led men to believe they could master the Mississippi, they also were the river's ally. They were bombs awaiting a spark, crude things trying to hold in with crude metal too much raw and awesome power.

The tenth Mississippi steamer, *George Washington*, was the first to blow up. Thirteen crewmen died that day in June 1816. By 1850 the same fate had claimed 185 boats. By 1860 the horror had been repeated on almost 200, and more than fifteen hundred persons had perished. One of the worst accidents was that of the *Louisiana*, whose boilers exploded at the New Orleans levee in 1849, killing eighty-six. The blast leveled to the waterline the two boats next to her.[15]

The original boilers were huge kettles with fireboxes underneath and steam receptacles above. Then, in 1862, Randolph Elder of Scotland, invented the marine fire-tube boiler which carried hot gasses from the firebox throughout the water in the boiler by dozens of tubes, or flues. The water was heated at many places inside the boiler rather than just from the bottom. The *Sultana* carried the more efficient boilers, and each of her four had twenty-four of the five-inch flues. It was soon found, however, that the boilers worked well and safely only on the upper portions of the Mississippi, where the water ran clear. Below Cairo, the Mississippi became muddy, filled with the washed-away soil of a vast land. The close-packed flues of the boilers became caked with sediment and scale, preventing the free circulation of water and causing rust. Worse, the mud and scale could cause dry pockets which, denied water, became red hot. In theory, if the sediment covering one of these superheated dry pockets broke loose, there would be an instantaneous generation of tremendously hot steam that no safety valve could vent in time. An explosion would occur. Therefore, fire-tube boilers used on the lower Mississippi had to be dismantled frequently and cleaned. The *Sultana*'s were so treated just before this trip, but now the thirst of the boilers was being slaked with unusually muddy water from the flooding Mississippi.[16]

As the pilot ruled in matters of navigation, the engineer ruled in matters concerning the engines. If Wintringer said the leaky boiler, the inside one of the left, or larboard, side, would have to be fixed, it would have to be done at the first opportunity. This meant Vicksburg.

Cass Mason could not have been aware of what awaited him at that Mississippi city. Major General Dana put Captain George A. Williams, departmental commissary of musters, in charge of supplying the camp and getting the exchanged prisoners aboard steamboats, thinking it would be a matter of a few hundred arriving at a time, who could be shipped up river in small groups as steamers arrived from downstream. Instead, Williams found himself swamped with more than a thousand men in the first batch from Cahaba. Soon nearly five thousand were crowded into an ill-prepared camp, forced to scratch as they had in prison for shelter and firewood, living off hardtack, dried meat, and pickled cabbage.[17]

Dana pressed Lieutenant Colonel Henderson to permit exchange of the prisoners, but Henderson could not, since few Confederate prisoners had arrived who could be swapped on the usual man-for-man basis. To release the men required authority from Richmond. But the Confederate capital by then had fallen to Grant and Colonel Robert Ould, the Confederate commissary general of prisoners, could not be located. Dana sent Williams to Mobile searching for someone who could give Henderson permission to declare the men exchanged. Captain Frederick Speed, assistant adjutant general of the department, volunteered to do Williams's work while he was gone, and Dana concurred. Ould was located at last and sent orders to Henderson to free the men. Speed began loading them on the first available steamboats, sending them on to Camp Chase in Ohio, where they would be mustered out of the service and returned to their families.[18]

A rumor surfaced that infuriated Speed and, on his return, Williams as well. It held that the Atlantic and Mississippi Steamship Company offered a bribe to Captain W. F. Kerns, assistant quartermaster in charge of transportation, to see that most of the men were loaded aboard company packets. At five dollars for each enlisted man and ten dollars for each officer, it could be a rich business. The rumor was reported to Dana, who told Speed he could do nothing without more evidence.[19]

By the time the *Sultana* put in at Vicksburg, many of the prisoners were gone, steaming north aboard the *Henry Ames*, the *Olive Branch*, and other vessels, none of which belonged to the Atlantic and Mississippi Steamship Company. However, the *Sultana* was expected to be joined at the Vicksburg landing by the *Pauline Carroll* and the *Lady Gay*, both vessels of the suspect company. Speed decided he would clear the camp of all remaining men and put them on the *Sultana*. He had not counted the men, however, to determine how many the *Sultana* would have to carry. He told Dana that it would be no more than 1,400, and the *Henry Ames* already had left with 1,300.[20]

Her boiler repaired by a local boilermaker, R. G. Taylor, the *Sultana* was getting up steam when the first released prisoners arrived.[21] They began crowding aboard as Williams wrote down their names and units. By railroad from the camp and by hurried march they arrived, and the steady stream became a crushing flood. Men from Kentucky, Michigan, Tennessee, Indiana, Virginia trooped aboard. They filled the main deck, poured up onto the upper decks and even crowded the roof of the texas. The promenade deck creaked and groaned. Chief mate William Rowberry led a crew of deck hands who began hammering stanchions under the sagging deck to keep it from collapsing. Despite the braces, the deck swayed downward.

Cass Mason became alarmed. His proud boat was being crushed underfoot. He stepped forward and halted the loading. He told Williams he would take no more. A prisoner heard Williams answer with profanity and say he was in charge and would put as many men aboard as he pleased.[22] The loading continued.

The men had been organized by units, but as they came up the gangplank they became mixed, and it was impossible for Williams to keep up. The exact number will never be known. Government records put the total at 1,866. F. A. Roziene of the Seventy-second Illinois and Joseph Elliott of an Indiana outfit, boarded early and counted in curiosity as the men crossed the gangplank. Roziene later reported 2,134 and Elliott 2,200. Several women from the U.S. Sanitary Commission, called the Christian Commission by the soldiers, climbed aboard to minister to the men.[23] The throng was joined also by a company of soldiers as escort.

A comparison of the incomplete passenger list and the records from the Bell Tavern hospital at Cahaba, which provide a nearly complete list of the Union regiments represented there, shows that well over 1,000 *Sultana* passengers may be identified as coming from the Alabama prison. Nine of the larger outfits on the *Sultana* also were the biggest at Cahaba and by themselves counted nearly 1,000 men among those known to be on the boat. They are the Third Tennessee, the 102nd Ohio, the Ninth Indiana, the

Fourth Kentucky, the Sixth Kentucky, the Second Michigan, the Eighteenth Michigan, the Fiftieth Ohio, and the 115th Ohio. A closer count is impossible since no one knew how many men were aboard and there is no exact count from the individual units. The passenger list, for example, includes only 304 from the Third Tennessee, yet it is known that 536 members of that regiment died during the war, only ten of them in combat. Twenty-one are known to have died at Cahaba, suggesting that many more than the listed 304 may have been aboard the *Sultana*. General Forrest, it should be remembered, captured 550 members of the regiment in the skirmishes at Athens and Sulphur Trestle on September 24 and September 25, 1864, all of them being sent to Cahaba.[24]

At about one o'clock in the morning of April 24, the *Sultana* moved slowly away. It took slightly more than thirty hours to reach Helena, where the photographer almost caused the boat to capsize. After an hour there, the packet headed toward Memphis, arriving at 7 P.M., April 26.

Six hours later she crossed to the Arkansas shore for fuel. Most of the passengers were asleep. The soldiers had been fed after a fashion, although the crush made meals nearly impossible. Some resorted to hardtack washed down with muddy river water. Others vented steam from the boilers to make coffee. A small stove was set up near the stern. There was salt pork but few could get to the stove to cook it. Still, most were happy. Crowding and privation might continue, but they were free and bound for home. A few had gone ashore at Memphis and were sleeping off their liquor. Some had earned money helping to unload part of the sugar in the hold. The *Sultana* passed in the blackness of the cloudy night an island group called Paddy's Hen and Chickens. Men noticed a thunderstorm building ahead.[25]

At about 2 A.M. on April 27, 1865, the *Sultana* had put Memphis eight miles to her stern, big paddle wheels churning the muddy water, tall stacks puffing black smoke. Then she erupted. One of her boilers exploded, as suddenly as a too-close jolt of lightning and thunder in the night, but louder and infinitely more terrifying. Then two other boilers, apparently weakened by the first blast, exploded. With terrible violence and horrible noise, with steam and people and debris and fire shooting skyward, she was torn apart. Dozens of men flew into the night sky at the first explosion, great chunks of wood and machinery with them, and for several seconds it rained people and wreckage. Many were broken or scalded and dead by the time they fell into the water. Others were so injured they could not swim and the water quickly claimed them. Others simply did not know how to swim and fought each other in their panic, drowning themselves and their companions. Men who would have given their lives to save another, claimed the lives of others in their desperate clutching at anything that would keep them from sinking. Some of the men fell back down onto the boat, some into the great hole blasted by the exploding boilers and into the exposed fire beds. Debris fell there, too, and as sudden as the explosion had been, fire lapped at the debris, feeding on the boat. The thunderstorm broke about the same time the boilers exploded, but its rain could not douse such an inferno.[26]

Supporting timbers throughout were split and cracked by the blasts. The pilothouse and cabins were shattered. Scalding steam and trampling feet killed as surely as the explosion. Hundreds began jumping overboard, and the water about the boat became a seething mass of desperate and panicked humanity. In the water and aboard the burning boat were screams and cries and shouts. The flames grew and men too hurt to move begged other men to throw them into the river that they might drown rather than burn. As Isaac Davenport, a veteran of Andersonville, put it in a letter, "Some men were drowning and some were burning and some were crying for help. Some were killed instantly, some were spared to [by] death and some borne away." He was rescued by men with a raft.[27]

Sergeant Aldrich was sleeping alongside a companion, J. W. Dunsmore, about midway on the cabin deck, when the explosion occurred.

Then first thing that I knew or heard was a terrible crash. Everything seemed to be falling. The things I had under my head, my shoes and some other articles tied up in an old pair of drawers, they went down through the floor. We scrambled back. The smoke came rushing up through the passage made by the exit of the exploded boilers. It was all confusion. The screams of women and children mingled with the groans of wounded and dying. Brave men rushed to and fro in the agony of fear, some uttering the most profane language and others commending their spirits to the Great Ruler of the Universe; the cries of the drowning and the roaring of the flames as they leaped upward made the scene most affecting and touching.[28]

Private Daniel Allen of the Third Tennessee Cavalry, another Cahaba man, was awakened in the stern of the main deck by the "shrieks and cries of the wounded and the terror stricken." He made his way toward the bow, pushing through the throng of the panicked and hurt, "passing many wounded sufferers who piteously begged to be thrown overboard." The horror was everywhere. "I saw men, while attempting to escape, pitch down through the hatchway that was full of blue curling flames."[29]

The fire spread rapidly, driving men, women, and children into the water where they clutched at each other and at anything within reach. Whole groups went down together, drowning together. The water was cold and many of the sick, weak, and injured suffered cramps and gave up. There was a wind from the north and for a while the dying steamboat remained pointing up stream, the paddle wheel housings acting as sails and the flames being blown toward the stern. Hundreds of people sought refuge on the bow until the paddle wheels burned away and the boat slowly turned in the wind. A mass of flames lashed the crowded bow, killing dozens with a sudden blast of heat and forcing the rest to jump into the water or burn.

James T. Wolverton, Company G, Sixth Tennessee Cavalry, a Cahaba man, was on the hurricane deck when the explosion occurred. "While drearily slumbering there all at once I felt a terrible shock followed by a deafening explosion, and before I could think my head struck water and I went down, down, struggling for breath." He grabbed a piece of the wreckage and another piece came to the surface between his legs. He floated with these all the way to Memphis where the lights "looked like hundreds of stars beckoning to us."[30]

Chester D. Berry remembered one of the women of the Christian Commission. She saw the men in the water fighting in the mad effort to save themselves, actually destroying each other and themselves in their struggles. She began talking to them, shouting above the roar of the flames and the cries and screams. She urged them to be men, to be calm. She succeeded in getting many quieted and directed them to cling to the ropes and chains hanging over the side. Then the flames began to close in on her. "The men pleaded and urged her to jump into the water and thus save herself, but she refused." She was afraid, Berry said, that she might panic and restart the mindless turmoil in the water. "And so, rather than run the risk of becoming the cause of the death of a single person, she folded her arms quietly over her bosom and burned, a voluntary martyr of the men she had lately quieted."[31]

Singly and in small groups, people began to escape the frantic throng of hundreds in the water around the boat and make their way downstream by floating, swimming, clinging to debris. Some struggled into the flooded timberlands along the shore where they clung to tree tops. There was no dry land they could reach. The flood covered the earth for miles and made the Mississippi an impossibly wide lake with a powerful current through the middle. Survivors reached what they thought were bushes only to find themselves at daylight holding onto the slender limbs of cottonwood trees whose tops were all that remained above the water.

Berry had just fallen asleep when the explosion occurred. He awoke to instant horror: the man lying next to him already was scalded to death. He picked up a piece of cabin door casing several inches wide and about four feet long and carried it against the moment when he would have to leave. "I did not want to take to the water just then, for it was literally black with human beings, many of them sinking and taking others with them." Even in the army he had never heard such swearing, praying, shouting, and crying, "and much of it from the same throat." Curses were followed by petitions to God, denunciations by bitter weeping. He came upon a man in helpless tears, wringing his hands as if in agony. "I'm not hurt at all, but I can't swim," he told Berry. "I've got to drown." Berry told him to secure a piece of wood to use as a float. "But I did get one, and someone snatched it away from me." Berry told him to get another. "I did, and they took that away from me." Berry told him to just get yet another. "Why, what would be the use? They would take it from me. Oh, dear, I tell you there is no use; I've got to drown. I can't swim." By this time Berry was disgusted and gave the weeping man a shove, telling him, "Drown then, you fool!" Twenty years later Berry would write, "I have been sorry all these years for that very act. . . . I have no doubt that he was drowned."[32]

Daniel McLeod, a former Union soldier discharged because of wounds, was one of the civilians who boarded at New Orleans. He was seated at a table when the boilers exploded. The heaving deck snapped both his ankles. He floated until rescued, but one of his legs had to be amputated.[33]

Perry Summerville, the youth who burned his crutches to start his cooking fires at Cahaba and could not bear to see the dead carried out of the Bell Tavern hospital, was one of those blown into the water. He had been asleep and knew nothing until he awoke in the river. He thought the boat had gone too close to shore and he had been dragged off by a tree limb. He began swimming toward the boat, shouting for help. "I had not gone far when I saw there was something the matter on board. I could see steam and fire and hear the screams." He found a rail from the boat, which kept him afloat. "I could see by the light from the burning boat as many as twenty go into the river at once." He saw a dead horse float by with six or eight men clinging to it. He was picked up by a man in a canoe who took him to a steamboat where he received medical attention and dry clothes. He had a chest injury and a badly scalded back. While he was on the rescue boat "a young man was brought in who was so badly scalded that his skin slipped off from the shoulders to the hands." Attendants covered the skinless arms of the young man with oil and "he walked the floor until a few minutes before his death."[34]

George F. Robinson, the Cahaba prisoner who escaped so many times with his friend John Corliss, was sleeping on the promenade deck between the stacks. He must have been stunned by the blast, for he knew nothing until he heard someone calling "For God's sake, cut the deck, I am burning to death." Robinson was covered with wreckage, and lying across his legs was his friend of so many adventures. John Corliss was dead. Robinson passed out, and came to as someone asked "What will I do? I cannot swim." Robinson looked about. "My God, what a sight!" he said later. "There were three or four hundred, all in a solid mass, in the water and all trying to get on top. I guess that nearly all were drowned." But that was not the worst he saw. Many were trapped in the wreckage and roasting in the flames. "Such screaming and yelling I never heard before or since."

Robinson joined the throng in the water but eluded the horde drowning together. He swam and floated until a mule drifted by. "I was almost a goner when I saw a dark object in the water and made for it, and it was a dead mule, one that was blown off the boat." The mule was not yet cold, and Robinson basked in the thin warmth still provided by the lifeless animal. He was rescued three miles below Memphis, unconscious but still clinging to his mule.[35]

John L. Walker, his friend Billy Morrow, and another man grabbed a gangplank to use as a float, "but before we could get it into the water every inch of space was seized by frantic men." It was pushed overboard "with its human freight." Walker stepped off before it went into the water "as I knew to remain meant sure death." When the plank struck the water "everyone was swept off, and never in my life have I witnessed such a struggle as there took place. . . . I thought the sights on the battlefields terrible, and they were, but they were not to be compared with the sights of that night when the animal nature of man came to the surface in the desperate struggle to save himself regardless of the life of others."[36]

Walker, who removed his clothes and shoes so he might swim more easily, was among those who took refuge on the bow until the boat turned and the blast of flame drove them overboard. "Being in about the center of the crowd I pushed those in front, those behind pushed us, and we all went into the river in a bunch. When I touched the water it was a great relief to my scorched body." He was driven under twice by people leaping upon him from the boat, but managed to find a piece of debris and float down to within about a mile of Memphis, where he was picked up by a steamboat.[37]

Stephen M. Gaston, the Indiana lad who was only fourteen when imprisoned at Cahaba, was one of those who helped unload the sugar at Memphis. He found a hogshead broken and took several pounds, eating about two pounds of the sugar before going to sleep in front of the pilothouse. "Our evening dreams were sweet . . . were we not going home to see our loved ones who had mourned for us as dead? We dreamed the soldier's dreams of home and loved ones, of camp life, of the battle and the prison, the scanty fare and the cruel guards."[38]

Gaston awoke as he was "raised to a height." Then he heard the thunderous explosion. One of the smoke stacks toppled onto the pilothouse, crushing it. The man next to him was dead. "Directly below some poor fellows were wedged in at my right and begged for help. . . . They soon smothered from the heat and smoke." He swung down to the lower deck on one of the support wires from the toppled stack. "Oh! God, what a sight. . . . Men were crying, praying, swearing, and begging. Wounded [were] in every shape, some with broken legs and arms, others scalded, burnt and dying." The cries, he said, "made the already dark night hideous, lighted up by the now fiercely burning boat." Gaston found an empty flour barrel and used it as a raft. Two or three men struggled toward it "but drowned before reaching me." He saw a group of at least twenty men drown together. He was picked up by a lifeboat from the steamer *Bostonia*.[39]

M. H. Sprinkle of the Sixteenth Ohio Volunteer Infantry, another Cahaba veteran, and a friend were busy with a terrible task before the fire drove them into the water. "Billy Lockhart and myself threw at least fifty of those who had been wounded in the explosion overboard, thinking it better that they should take their chances of drowning than be left to burn up."[40]

Slowly help began to arrive. Men would remember a Confederate lieutenant who appeared out of the darkness riding a dugout canoe. Frank Barkton had been camping out on the distant shore. He worked night-long pulling men aboard his little craft and paddling them to safety. Back and forth he traveled until there were no more to save.[41]

Steamboats heading for New Orleans came upon the wreck and began pulling survivors aboard. The ironclad gunboat *Essex* at Memphis sent its crew out in small boats. The *Bostonia* dropped anchor near the wreckage and pulled a hundred aboard.[42]

When Chester Berry at last went into the water, he heard the crash of breaking timbers behind him. He looked back. The covering of one of the paddle wheels had broken away just as a soldier stepped onto it. The man began to fall between the cover and the boat when the housing snapped back against him and penned him "as in an iron vice" for the flames leaping from below. "Even now," Berry wrote, "after the lapse of years, it almost seems as though I could hear the poor fellow's screams as the forked flames swept around him."[43]

That terrible scene had been before the paddle wheels and their coverings burned away and allowed the boat to slowly turn in the wind so that the flames could reach the bow and the hundreds who had taken refuge there. After that, there were no more aboard the boat who lived. What was left of the once-elegant river queen drifted over to near the Arkansas shore and spun for a time in an eddy, burning to the waterline.

The rescued were taken to Memphis. They were pitifully few considering the more than 2,000 aboard. About 520 were hospitalized, and more than 200 of these died. The Gayoso hospital received 138, the Adams 139, the Washington 143, the Overton 90, the Officers' 6, and the Webster and the Soldiers' Home a few more.[44] These hospitals had been established to support Grant's campaign against Vicksburg. Their last major function before closing down was to help freed prisoners of war who began their trip homeward at that same Mississippi River city.

Among the dead out on the dark river was Captain Cass Mason. The river kept his body. Among the dead also was Corporal Edwin Ford who wrote home to Hillsdale, Michigan, about how well fed he was at Cahaba Federal Prison. Among the living were Big Tennessee, nemesis of the Cahaba muggers, and Nathan Wintringer, the Sultana's chief engineer. He blamed the explosion on the fire-tube boilers. Afterward, he said, the boiler repaired at Vicksburg was found largely intact in the burned wreckage. It was the only one of the four that did not explode.[45]

How many died will never be known. Brigadier General William Hoffman, assigned to investigate, placed the loss at 1,238, a ridiculous figure. Official totals released by the U.S. Customs Service listed 1,547, but the true number may well have been more than 1,600.[46] All the hundreds of steamboat accidents that occurred before on the western rivers hardly claimed together as many lives as did the *Sultana*.

The Mississippi still was not finished. She buried the wreckage in mud and changed her course, and no man could say later exactly where it happened, could not even mark a true spot for remembering.

10
Call Loud the
Muster Roll

The small steamer *Jenny Lind* set out from Memphis every day for two weeks, visiting the spot near the Arkansas shore where the charred remains of the *Sultana* lay, so that men might recover bodies as they came to the surface. The river kept most of the dead, although some were fished from the water as far south as Helena, ninety miles away. The Memphis *Daily Bulletin* reported on May 27 that 197 had been brought in and buried. Rewards were posted for the remains of Captain Mason and a few others, but went unclaimed. A drive to benefit the survivors produced only $1,183.90 and was given to 23 of those the fund-raising committee thought suffered most, the shares ranging from $10 to $200.[1]

The nation little noticed the tragedy that the Memphis *Argus* called "the most appalling disaster in the marine annals of America, if not the world." The New York *Times* carried its first story on Saturday, April 29. The worst accident of any sort in United States history rated only five column inches on page four. "Dreadful Disaster," said the headlines. "Explosion of a Mississippi Steamer—Fourteen

Hundred Lives supposed to be lost." On the following days the *Times* included accounts taken from other newspapers. However, the *Sultana* did not make the front page until May 3, six days after the horror. Then the editors moved the story back to the inside pages on the following day, and afterward mentioned the *Sultana* no more. Most newspapers handled the story in like fashion, and the New York *Herald* was no more interested than the *Times*.[2]

Harper's Weekly provided a brief account on May 13, running it as the second item, after a summary of the military situation, in a page-three column labeled "Domestic Intelligence." The story was an excerpt from the one carried in the Memphis *Daily Bulletin* the day after the accident. It said: "The scene following the explosion was heartrending and terrible in the extreme. Hundreds of people were blown into the air, and descending into the water, some dead, some with broken limbs, some scalded, were borne under by the resistless current of the great river, never to rise again. The survivors represent the screams as agonizing beyond precedent."[3]

Harper's printed a woodcut of the tragedy on May 20, an artist's conception of the great burning steamboat surrounded by a mass of people struggling in the dark river.[4] After that, it ignored the *Sultana*. Too much that bore more heavily on the nation's life happened too swiftly for the *Sultana* to be of more than temporary concern for those whose lives were not touched directly. Sharing the headlines of the newspapers of the days immediately following the accident were the accelerating collapse of the Confederacy; the aftermath of Lincoln's assassination, and the long, slow movement of his funeral train west; the death of his assassin; the hunt for Jefferson Davis; and fear of the powerful and elusive Confederate warship *Stonewall*. There simply was too great a rush of too many major events; too much after four years of too much.

The *Sultana* burns while victims struggle in the Mississippi. This is the woodcut printed by *Harper's Weekly* on May 20, 1865.

Even the investigations were fairly quiet. Major General Dana, who should have seen to the safe transport of the soldiers, held Captain Speed accountable for overloading the boat. A court-martial convicted Speed and sentenced him to a dishonorable discharge. He was the only one prosecuted. On review, Judge Advocate General Joseph Holt recommended on June 21, 1866, that the conviction be overturned on grounds that Speed had nothing to do with the explosion and faced punishment too harsh for the mistake of merely overloading a steamboat. He was reinstated and mustered out of the service routinely and honorably the following year.[5]

Rumors circulated that someone secreted a bomb inside a lump of the fuel the *Sultana* took aboard at the coal yard across the river from Memphis. Such tales persisted for more than twenty years, but few believed them, and the official reports blamed the disaster on the boilers. After additional explosions, which destroyed the *Walker R. Carter* and the *Missouri*, the fire-tube boilers were banned on the lower, muddier stretches of the Mississippi where a buildup of mud and scale on the flues turned engines into bombs.[6]

Late in 1885, survivors held a convention in Fostoria, Ohio, and Chester D. Berry, by then a minister, collected the material for his book. He published it in 1892, and even then there was confusion over how many died. On the title page he called the book the "History of a disaster where over one thousand five hundred human beings were lost." In the foreword, he gave the figure as over 1,700. Either could be correct, and the truth must forever remain elusive.

William H. Norton of Company C, 115th Ohio, entertained the convention with a poem, and a few lines give something of the mood and the memories.

> The sleeping soldiers dream of home,
> To them the long-sought day had come,
> No more in prison pens to moan.
> On sails the steamer through the gloom,
> On sleep the soldiers to their doom,
> And death's dark angel—oh! so soon—
> Calls loud the muster-roll.[7]

The final muster was called on the dark river that chilly April night, and in the hospitals of Memphis on the following days, for just-released prisoners of war from Tennessee, Kentucky, Indiana, Ohio, Michigan, and Virginia. A thousand or more of them were Cahaba men, although it is not possible to arrive at an exact figure. The contingent from East Tennessee, almost all veterans of Castle Morgan, was devastated. Of its hundreds, including most of the Third Tennessee Cavalry, only sixty-eight survived.[8]

Not all the prisoners at Cahaba left when the gates opened. Nineteen remained in Bell Tavern, too sick to begin the journey home, and were there on April 27, the day the *Sultana* explosion killed their companions. The following day, however, all but three were well enough to travel and were released. That is the day Private Samuel Cooke of the Fourth Kentucky Cavalry died of diarrhea and became the last Union victim of Cahaba Federal Prison, the 142nd name on the surgeons' report labeled Deaths Among Federals. The other two men were released the next day, and Cahaba had served its final moment as the site of a prison camp.[9]

An investigation began that summer into the disappearance and presumed murder of Captain Hiram Hanchett, the leader of the Cahaba mutiny. The officer in charge of the probe concluded that "Captain Hanchett was foully dealt with and put to death either by [Lieutenant Colonel] Jones and his adjutant, his orders or by his knowledge."[10] By the summer, though, it was too late to capture Jones or Lieutenant Robinson, his adjutant. They were posted to Demopolis when the prisoners left Castle Morgan, and remained there until the war ended. Jones was visible and active, not yet fearing a Yankee noose. He may have had ample funds for his later escape. He reported in a dispatch to department headquarters on May 1 that he had a package of money spirited from the Selma arsenal before the city fell to Wilson's cavalry on the same day that Richmond fell to Grant. The money, he said, was brought to him by a Lieutenant Compton, a friend and officer of the arsenal. He had not counted it, but it was supposed to be from $100,000 to $200,000. He asked whether he could use it to pay the expenses of his post. On May 5 he reported he still had the funds. No answer to his message arrived.

If the money was in Confederate dollars, as seems most likely, it was worthless.

On May 6 Lieutenant General Richard Taylor announced surrender of his command, which included Demopolis, to Major General Edward R. S. Canby, and instructed all to cease the struggle. The last message from Jones was sent on May 9 asking whether he and his men might surrender at Demopolis or Selma rather than go to Meridian, the department headquarters.[11] Apparently they could not, for Jones signed his third and final parole as a surrendered Confederate soldier at Meridian on May 17, 1865, signing as he did everything, maintaining to the last his ties to his beloved Twenty-Second: "S. Jones, Lt. Col., 22nd La. Regt." It is history's last word from Lieutenant Colonel Jones. It promised, "The above named officer will not be disturbed by United States authorities as long as he observes his parole and the laws in force where he resides."[12]

Federal authorities most assuredly wanted to disturb Jones once they learned of Captain Hanchett's disappearance. They sought him for more than a year. They were told in Cahaba that he might be found in New Orleans, but a search was fruitless. Jones could have fled from that bustling port to the still-wild West, or anywhere in the world he wished. Among his suspected accomplices, investigators apprehended only unimportant P. B. Vaughn, and in August 1866 they decided little would be served by punishing him alone. They turned the investigation over to Alabama authorities, and the Federal government's probe into the apparent death of Captain Hanchett ended.[13] No trace of him ever was found; no one was ever punished.

Lieutenant Colonel Henderson received a signal honor in the closing days of the war, by his own account at least. When he helped establish Camp Fisk, Union officers thought the Confederate, whose kindnesses to Union prisoners they knew well, deserved protection while he handled his duties in the area both sides declared neutral. They assigned a battalion of the Ninth Indiana Cavalry as a bodyguard, and the man in gray rode at the head of men in blue. They were loyal, and he had need of them on a sad night in April.

Several officers of both sides were at Henderson's headquarters that night, entertaining each other with stories and card tricks. A Federal orderly arrived with a large envelope tied in black ribbon, the first news of Lincoln's assassination. A distraught Federal surgeon, seeing southern conspiracy behind the tragedy, drew his saber in rage, ready to attack the Confederates there. A Rebel major immediately yanked his pistol from its holster and aimed at the surgeon, ordering him to resheathe his blade. Calm was restored and Union Major Frank E. Miller assured Henderson, "I will protect you if I have to sacrifice myself."

It was a most dangerous time for the Confederates, for they were few, and the area held many thousands of Union troops and prisoners of war who might want to take revenge with the lives of southerners. Henderson sent for Major Wall, who commanded his bodyguard, telling him to bring an escort of twenty mounted men and horses for the Confederate staff. "In less than ten minutes the major and the detail reported. I asked him who he regarded as his commander. He answered: 'You, sir!' I then told him of the tragedy, and inquired whether he was ready to deliver us at General Dana's headquarters, where I would ask for protection. He replied, 'I will as faithfully obey your orders as if you were General Dana himself.' "

General Dana offered Henderson and his staff a locomotive for a predawn dash to the Big Black River where they would be ferried to the Confederate side, guarded by Texas Rangers. They made the run safely right through thousands of Federal prisoners of war at Camp Fisk, Henderson and his staff riding on the locomotive's tender. A boat landed them safely on the shore held by the Rangers. Henderson felt safe as soon as he saw them. "A score of Texas Rangers, their long, unkempt hair flowing from beneath their sombreros, reddened like Mephistopheles in 'Faust' by the glare of the camp fires freshly fueled, stood around, walking arsenals. The scene reminded me of some of the situations depicted in Dante's 'Inferno.' "

The Texans were saddened by the news of Lincoln. "I never heard one of those fierce-looking frontiersmen utter a mean or malignant expression," Henderson wrote. "All felt that an awful blow had been struck the fainting fortunes of the South."

The next day, Henderson had the Confederate colors flown at half-staff, and the flags of both North and South mourned on opposite sides of the river. In less than a week it was safe to return to Camp Fisk, and General Dana sent a special train for Henderson. The southerners draped Confederate headquarters at Fisk in the black of mourning and they "were so clothed when the star of the Confederacy . . . set in rayless night."[14]

Henderson and Colonel Watts sent a letter to General Dana to "Express their sincere regrets occasioned by receipt of the painful intelligence of the assassination of President Lincoln and Secretary Seward." They told the general that "no officer of the United States Government regrets more than they this cowardly assault upon these high officers of state, and the introduction of this tragical chapter into American history." They said they hoped it would not interrupt the prisoner exchanges. General Dana replied the following day, April 19, to "express my high appreciation of the honorable sentiments." He promised "no lessening of the courtesy and friendliness which have made our recent intercourse under flag of truce so entirely satisfactory."[15]

Henderson afterward returned to Demopolis, his prewar home where he had been a minister, and became editor of the Demopolis *New Era*. He wrote editorials calling for industrialization of the South and criticizing the Union for such deeds as outlawing monuments to southern valor. He remained staunchly a Confederate in those first months after the war and saw much danger for the South in the possibility of northern revenge. Writing back to his newspaper from a trip home to Millersburg, Kentucky, Henderson said in the edition of October 3, 1866: "The people in the South must be patient and prayerful. They are bound hand and foot. . . . We must wait with time and patience, and not exhaust our moral force by craven admissions to exacting power and in useless repinings. . . . God in goodness may yet rebuke the folly and fanaticism of the North, but from present indications the Devil seems turned loose for a season."[16]

Henderson sent his wife and daughter to Millersburg late in the war, and there they remained while he edited the *New Era*. During the family's separation, death took Henderson's daughter, the child much petted by the Cahaba prisoners.[17] In the edition of August 8, 1866, he included a letter from his wife announcing Ada's death. A touching account told how the townspeople insisted on her burial in a section of the cemetery reserved for Methodist ministers, since he had been one before the war. Apparently moved by the gesture, Henderson resigned from the *New Era* and went home to resume the ministry.

He served churches in Frankfort and Lexington, and then entered politics. In 1871 he won election to the first of his consecutive terms as superintendent of public instruction in Kentucky, winning by 43,598 votes over his nearest rival. His tenure was noted for establishment of schools for blacks and for improvements to the physical plant of Kentucky schools. He also was professor of literature at the Kentucky Military Institute. Afterward, he took charge of the Southern Methodist Church in San Francisco, and he served churches in Hannibal, Missouri; Jersey City, New Jersey; and in Cincinnati and other Ohio cities.[18]

It may appear strange that a southern Methodist accepted a church in New Jersey, but Major Frank Miller, the Union officer who pledged to sacrifice himself for Henderson at Camp Fisk, became a Presbyterian pastor at Paterson, New Jersey, and may have had something to do with the move. Henderson certainly admired him, writing that he was a "Christian gentleman . . . full of high-erected thoughts in a heart of courtesy."[19] Henderson's congregation at Jersey City's Simpson Church included the mother and two sisters of General Grant, as noted in Chapter 3. After the death of his father, the general's mother moved to New York to live with one of her daughters, who had married a New York businessman. On Sundays, the family crossed the Hudson River from Manhattan to hear Henderson's sermons in the church that bore the name of Mrs. Grant's family. So it was that the former southern prison commander was called upon to conduct the funeral services of the general's mother.[20]

Henderson took an active interest in Freemasonry and was grand chaplain of the Grand Lodge of Kentucky. He edited the *Kentucky Freemason*, and also became involved in Odd Fellowship, serving as grand master of the order in Kentucky. He retired to Cincinnati and became chaplain of the First Regiment of the Ohio National Guard. He served with it during the Spanish-American War, becoming a U.S. soldier late in April 1898 and being mustered out with the regiment the following October 25. On Tuesday, January 16, 1912, Henderson died at Christ Hospital in Cincinnati at the age of seventy-five. He was buried at Frankfort, Kentucky.[21]

The Cincinnati *Enquirer* honored Henderson with a

lengthy obituary, but incorrectly said he was a Confederate brigadier general and did not mention his command at one of the infamous southern prison camps. That was not mentioned, either, by the state-published *History of Education in Kentucky*, which dealt at length with his contributions.[22]

Among the Federal soldiers who survived Castle Morgan and the *Sultana*, the histories of a few may be mentioned. John Walker became a plumber and founded the John L. Walker Company, a plumbing, steam-heating, and electrical concern in Hamilton, Ohio. He died on August 3, 1910. Perry Summerville became a farmer at Brazil, Indiana. George Robinson, the persistent escapee, became a shoe clerk in Owosso, Michigan. Alonzo A. Van Vlack, who suffered so badly from scurvy, farmed outside Cambria, Michigan. Daniel Garber made shoes for about ten years and then turned to farming at Butler, Ohio. There he raised four girls and three boys. Chester D. Berry became a minister at Tekonsha, Michigan.[23]

Jesse Hawes, who was not aboard the *Sultana*, became a doctor in Colorado. Drummer George Tod and Melvin Grigsby, of course, survived Andersonville and also were not on the *Sultana*. Grigsby moved to Sioux Falls and raised two boys. Tod left Iowa for his native Pennsylvania and passed from view.[24]

Some of them outlived by many years their prison town of Cahaba, the town that began as Alabama's first state capital. Shortly after the war it lost the honor of being even the county seat. The last flood, the one that added to the misery of the three thousand prisoners just before their release, was the final blow to luckless Cahaba. The county seat was moved to Selma, and Cahaba entered its final chapter. Within twenty years too little remained to merit marking on a map.

In modern times, Alabamians began to observe Cahaba Days, to have fun and celebrate the memory of the first

Call Loud the Muster Roll 149

capital. The prison virtually was forgotten, the only reminder a historic marker in the middle of the dirt lane that had been Capitol Street. The marker pointed to the wrong side of the street, to the wrong site. A small barbecue stand was built and a gasoline pump installed. A tall sign on the river bank advertised fuel for the motorboats that churn noisily on the river, and stood over the hidden bones and buttons of a long-ago soldier. Unknown to the fun-seekers who attended the annual Cahaba Days, the area chosen for their picnic tables and games was precisely the ground where the old prison stood, the ground of Big Tennessee, Captain Hanchett, Jesse Hawes, Perry Summerville, little Stephen Gaston, tiny drummer-boy George Tod, and so many others. Even the barbecue stand would have been within the prison stockade.

Finally the state bought the place and rediscovered the true site of the prison. The barbecue stand, the gasoline pump, and the advertising sign came down. The whole area, town and prison, is to be preserved, to become part of a state park. It is supposed to continue as a place of entertainment and fun on the banks of a now-dammed and sluggish Alabama River. It also will be a place, however, for learning a little about the past, a place for remembering, and now the soldiers will be included.

Following the *Sultana* disaster, the Mississippi shifted about three miles eastward and the site of the explosion became dry land. For many years pieces of the wreckage, near Mound City, Arkansas, could be seen, but floods buried it and the exact place was lost to memory. Now a Memphis lawyer, Jerry Potter, and Samuel Oliver, a farmer from Marion, Arkansas, say they know where the remains of the old steamboat lie under twenty feet of black dirt in a field usually devoted to soybeans. It is not known when, or if, recovery will be attempted.[25]

A huge live oak once stood on the Alabama's bank at

Cahaba, so old as to have cooled De Soto's soldiers in its wide shade. When most of the trees were cut in the building of the town, the woodsmen spared the majestic old oak. Legend has it that while Spanish moss and mistletoe grew abundantly on the other remaining trees, they did not touch this one. The townspeople held the giant in awe. They said that at times its evergreen leaves trembled from some internal agitation although the air was still. Some disaster, they said, always followed the trembling. During the flood in March 1865, just before the prisoners left for Vicksburg and the *Sultana* during those painful last days of the Confederacy, the water washed away the soil supporting the tree, and the old monarch of centuries fell crashing at last into the river and was swept away. People said a most violent shaking of its leaves occurred a few days before.[26]

Notes

1. The Civil War and Its Prisons

1. J. G. Randall and David Herbert Donald, *The Civil War and Reconstruction* (Lexington, Mass.: D. C. Heath, 1969), 193n; Douglas Southall Freeman, *R. E. Lee: A Biography,* 4 vols. (New York: Charles Scribner's Sons, 1936), 3:5. Confederates killed, wounded, and captured at Chancellorsville totaled 13,156. William Best Hesseltine, *Civil War Prisons: A Study in War Psychology* (Columbus: Ohio State University Press, 1930), 152n. The National Cemetery at Andersonville includes the graves of 12,912 prisoners who died there. Francis Trevelyan Miller, ed., *The Photographic History of the Civil War,* 10 vols. (New York: Thomas Yoseloff, 1957), 10:144; Thomas L. Livermore, *Numbers and Losses in the Civil War in America, 1861–65* (Boston: Houghton, Mifflin, 1901), 102–103. The Gettysburg figures are 23,049 casualties for the North and 28,063 for the South.

2. Randall and Donald, *The Civil War and Reconstruction,* 190, 193n. The Union's population was 20,700,000 and the South's 9,105,000, including 3,654,000 blacks, all but a relatively small number of them slaves.

152

3. Ibid., 190, 255; Robert C. Black III, *The Railroads of the Confederacy* (Chapel Hill: University of North Carolina Press, 1952), 13–14.

4. Map accompanying Black, *The Railroads of the Confederacy*.

5. Freeman, *Lee*, 3:252, 253.

6. I. A. Newby, *The South: A History* (New York: Holt, Rinehart & Winston, 1978), 224; Stewart Brooks, *Civil War Medicine* (Springfield, Ohio: Charles C. Thomas, 1966), 68, 70; *The War of the Rebellion: A Compilation of the Official Records of the Union and Confederate Armies* (hereinafter cited as *OR*), Ser. 4, 2:1024; Howard L. Holley, *The History of Medicine in Alabama* (Birmingham: University of Alabama School of Medicine, 1982), 139. Dr. Norman J. Doorenbos of Auburn University, whose Ph.D. is in medicinal chemistry, believes Surgeon General Moore's quinine substitute had about the same effect as aspirin. He said the bark of willow and poplar contains substances the body would metabolize into salicylic acid, which is aspirin. The dogwood bark offered little medicinal value, however. Anna M. Gayle Fry, "Life in Dallas County During the War," *Confederate Veteran*, 24 (May 1916): 216–22.

7. Freeman, *Lee*, 3:251.

8. James Lee McDonough and James Pickett Jones, *War So Terrible* (New York: W. W. Norton, 1987), 55–56.

9. *OR*, Ser. 2, 8:588.

10. Ibid., 624.

11. Ibid., 153, 175, 803, are examples of the treatment accorded black soldiers.

12. Ibid., 7:607.

13. Ibid., 614–15.

14. William F. Fox, *Regimental Losses in the American Civil War* (Albany: Albany Publishing Company, 1889), 524; Paul E. Steiner, *Disease in the Civil War* (Springfield, Ohio: Charles C. Thomas, 1968), 37.

15. Hesseltine, *Civil War Prisons*, 256n; Bruce Catton, "Prison Camps of the Civil War," *American Heritage* (August 1959): 4–8, 96–97.

16. Hesseltine, *Civil War Prisons*, 159, 256n.

17. Miller, *Photographic History*, 7:60–61; James L. Conrad,

"Held Captive at Cahaba," *Civil War Times Illustrated* (November 1982): 12–19. Peter A. Brannon, "The Cahawba Military Prison, 1863–1865," *Alabama Review* (July 1950): 163–67.

18. Jesse Hawes, *Cahaba: A Story of Captive Boys in Blue* (New York: Burr Printing House, 1888).

19. Hesseltine, *Civil War Prisons*, 159, 252; Hawes, *Cahaba*, 462; Lewis W. Day, *The Story of the One Hundred and First Ohio Infantry* (Cleveland, Ohio: W. M. Bayne Printing Co., 1894), 342; *OR*, Ser. 2, 8:493.

20. Chester D. Berry, *Loss of the Sultana and Reminiscences of Survivors* (Lansing, Mich.: Darius D. Thorp, 1892); James Elliott, *Transport to Disaster* (New York: Holt, Rinehart & Winston, 1962).

2. The Town and Its Prison

1. Walter M. Jackson, *The Story of Selma* (Birmingham: Birmingham Printing, 1954), 104; Deed Book S, 724, Deed Book T, 240, 400, Dallas County Courthouse, Selma.

2. Anna M. Gayle Fry, *Memories of Old Cahaba* (Nashville: Publishing House of the Methodist Episcopal Church, South, 1908), 26; *OR*, Ser. 4, 1:1089–91, 1171–73, 2:486; Black, *Railroads of the Confederacy*, 33, 154.

3. Interview, October 5, 1986, with Linda Derry, archaeologist employed by the Alabama Historical Commission as manager of the Old Cahawba Preservation Project.

4. Henderson's military records, National Archives.

5. *OR*, Ser. 2, 6:1124; Hawes, *Cahaba*, 13–14; Fry, *Memories*, 21.

6. Selma *Morning Reporter*, March 29, 1864; *OR*, Ser. 1, 31, Pt. 3:673; Selma *Morning Reporter*, April 11, 1864.

7. *OR*, Ser. 2, 6:1124–25.

8. J. D. Harwell, "In and Around Vicksburg," *Confederate Veteran*, 30 (September 1922): 333–34.

9. Hesseltine, *Civil War Prisons*, 135; *OR*, Ser. 2, 7:76, 110.

10. Selma *Morning Reporter*, May 13, 1864.

11. *OR*, Ser. 2, 7:998–1002.

12. Miller, ed., *The Photographic History*, 7:141.

13. Melvin Grigsby, *The Smoked Yank* (Sioux Falls: Dakota Bell, 1888), 80; Deed Book AA, 481, Deed Book KK, 214, Dallas County Courthouse, Selma.

14. *Rivers of Alabama* (Huntsville, Ala.: Strode, 1958), 123–30. Information was provided by the Cahaba Historical Commission and was included in a pamphlet published without date by the Tourist and Convention Committee of the Selma and Dallas County Chamber of Commerce.

15. *Rivers of Alabama*, 128.

16. William H. Brantley, *Three Capitals: A Book about the First Three Capitals of Alabama, St. Stephens, Huntsville, & Cahawba* (1947; reprint ed., University: University of Alabama Press, 1976), 61.

17. Unpublished Craig family papers provided by Dr. John M. Jackson, a descendant, of Eufaula, Alabama.

18. U.S. Census, Dallas County, Alabama, 1860.

19. Fry, *Memories*, 13, 25.

20. *Rivers of Alabama*, 129; Fry, *Memories*, 14.

21. Brantley, *Three Capitals*, 167–68; Fry, *Memories*, 14, 17–18; W. Brewer, *Alabama: Her History, Resources, War Record, and Public Men* (Montgomery: Barrett & Brown, 1872), 208, 209; Census, Dallas County, 1860.

22. Linda Derry, interview, October 5, 1986; Brantley, *Three Capitals*, 65.

23. *OR*, Ser. 2, 7:445–46.

24. Ibid., 446.

25. Black, *Railroads of the Confederacy*, map in back; *OR*, Ser. 2, 7:448.

26. *OR*, Ser. 2, 7:458, 469.

27. Ibid., 458, 467.

28. Ibid., 678.

29. Ibid., 773, 998–1002; Hesseltine, *Civil War Prisons*, 154–56.

30. Hawes, *Cahaba*, 158.

31. *OR*, Ser. 2, 7:998–1002.

32. Fry, *Memories*, 53.

33. *OR*, Ser. 2, 7:1002.

34. Linda Derry, interview, October 5, 1986.

35. *OR*, Ser. 2, 7:1088.

36. Ibid., 1088–89.

37. Ibid., 1014, 1081; Hawes, *Cahaba*, 277, 346–47; William Stanley Hoole, ed., "The Battle of Athens and Letters from Cahawba Prison, 1864–1865," *Alabama Review*, 15 (January 1962): 151; Record Group 249, "Register of Federal Prisoners of War at Confederate Prison Hospital, Cahaba, Ala." (hereinafter cited as Register, National Archives), 374–96, 398–403, 407–20. Page 408 shows 110 Federal men were released from the hospital on November 21, 1864.

3. The Commanders

1. Hawes, *Cahaba*, 252–58; Grigsby, *The Smoked Yank*, 74; William M. Armstrong, "Cahaba to Charleston: The Prison Odyssey of Lt. Edmund E. Ryan," *Civil War History* (June 1962): 218–21; John L. Walker, *Cahaba Prison and the Sultana Disaster* (Hamilton, Ohio: Brown & Whitaker, 1910), 18; Howard A. M. Henderson, "Lincoln's Assassination and Camp Fisk," *Confederate Veteran*, 15 (April 1907): 170–71; *OR*, Ser. 2, 7:1176–77, 1205.

2. Ishbel Ross, *The General's Wife* (New York: Dodd, Mead, 1959), 281; *History of Education in Kentucky* (Frankfort: Kentucky Department of Education, 1914), 119–20; Henderson's military records, National Archives.

3. Hawes, *Cahaba*, 259–60; *OR*, Ser. 2, 8:794–95, 834–35, 951, 7:998, 6:203.

4. Hawes, *Cahaba*, 258; military records of Lieutenant Colonel Sam Jones, National Archives, Washington, D.C.; *OR*, Ser. 1, 6:521–34, 548.

5. Jones's military records, National Archives.

6. *OR*, Ser. 1, 24, Pt. 2:328; Jones's military records, National Archives. A brief sketch of his military career through 1863 also may be found in *Records of Louisiana Confederate Soldiers and Louisiana Confederate Commands*, 3 vols. (Spartanburg, S.C.: Reprint Co., 1984), 3, Bk. 1:476–77. The original was published in New Orleans in 1920 and does not include Jones's court-martial, assignment to Cahaba, or that he was sought after the war on a charge of murder. Jones's military records, National Archives.

7. Jones to Jack, March 19, 1864, Jones's military records, National Archives.

8. Ibid. The surviving records, while incomplete, are clear on Jones's alteration of the muster roll and the court's decision.

9. Ibid., March 3, 1864, Jones's military records, National Archives. The file includes several other letters by Jones in a similar vein. They are not included here because they would amount largely to mere repetition.

10. Report of staff officers serving at the Post of Cahaba, Jones's military records, National Archives; *OR*, Ser. 1, 39, Pt. 2:809, 49:1206–15, passim.

11. *OR*, Ser. 2, 7:1051.

12. Ibid., Ser. 1, 49, Pt. 2:1273.

13. Ibid., Ser. 2, 7:1001.

14. Jones's military records, National Archives.

15. Henderson's military records, National Archives; *History of Education in Kentucky*, 119–20; Demopolis *New Era*, August 8, 1866; John Witherspoon DuBose, "Chronicles of the Canebrake," manuscript in the Alabama State Archives, Montgomery, 117.

16. DuBose, "Chronicles of the Canebrake," 119; Henderson's military records, National Archives.

17. Hawes, *Cahaba*, 259, 260.

18. Hosea C. Aldrich, *Cahawba Prison: A Glimpse of Life in a Rebel Prison* (n.p., n.d.), 6; also Hosea C. Aldrich, "Cahawba Prison, Alabama," *Camp-Fire Sketches and Battle-Field Echoes of the Rebellion by 'The Boys'* (n.p., n.d.), 241–43; Hawes, *Cahaba*, 448.

19. Walker, *Cahaba Prison*, 13.

20. Emmet C. West, *History and Reminiscences of the Second Wisconsin Cavalry Regiment* (Portage, Wis.: State Register Print, 1914), 31.

21. Hawes, *Cahaba*, 252, 254, 255–56, 258.

22. Ibid., 252–54.

23. Walker, *Cahaba Prison*, 18.

24. Fry, "Life in Dallas County During the War," 221.

25. Hawes, *Cahaba*, 259.

26. Hoole, ed., "The Battle of Athens and Letters from Cahawba Prison, 1864–1865," 151.

4. The Men

1. Grigsby, *The Smoked Yank*, 74.

2. Ibid.

3. Ibid., 74–75.

4. Ryan's diary, Peoria Historical Society, Peoria, Illinois; William M. Armstrong, "Cahaba to Charleston: The Prison Odyssey of Lt. Edmund E. Ryan," *Civil War History* (June 1962): 219–21. The latter also was in *Civil War Prisons*, edited by William Best Hesseltine, published in 1962 by Kent State University.

5. *OR*, Ser. 2, 6:1124.

6. Grigsby, *The Smoked Yank*, 75–76; Hawes, *Cahaba*, 271; Ovid Futch, "Prison Life at Andersonville," in *Civil War Prisons*, Hesseltine, ed., 27–28; originally in *Civil War History*, 8, no. 2 (1962).

7. Hawes, *Cahaba*, 154–55, 480; Day, *The Story of the One Hundred and First Ohio Infantry*, 342; Walker, *Cahaba Prison*, 6; Fry, *Memories*, 36; *OR*, Ser. 2, 7:1001, 1177.

8. *OR*, Ser. 2, 6:1124, 7:1002, 8:596; Hawes, *Cahaba*, 15, 160.

9. *OR*, Ser. 4, 2:1011–12. This is a discussion of the tax in kind contained in a lengthy report from Secretary of War James A. Seddon to President Jefferson Davis, dated November 26, 1863. Ser. 2, 7:1000; Fry, "Life in Dallas County During the War," 217.

10. *OR*, Ser. 2, 7:999; Aldrich, *Cahawba Prison*, 3.

11. Hawes, *Cahaba*, 206.

12. Ibid., 204, 208, 209; Walker, *Cahaba Prison*, 6; Aldrich, *Cahawba Prison*, 3.

13. Walker, *Cahaba Prison*, 1, 9.

14. Hoole, ed., "The Battle of Athens and Letters from Cahawba Prison, 1864–1865," 151, 152.

15. Ibid., 150.

16. *OR*, Ser. 2, 7:1082.

17. Selma *Morning Reporter*, April 2, 1864; Brannon, "The Cahawba Military Prison," 167.

18. Hawes, *Cahaba*, 129; Walker, *Cahaba Prison*, 5–6; Conrad, "Held Captive at Cahaba," 17.

19. Aldrich, *Cahawba Prison*, 4; Hawes, *Cahaba*, 273.

20. *OR*, Ser. 2, 7:1000; Day, *The Story of the One Hundred and First Ohio Infantry*, 342.

21. Hawes, *Cahaba*, 151; Walker, *Cahaba Prison*, 9; Day, *The Story of the One Hundred and First Ohio Infantry*, 342; Register, 414; Bert Neville, *A Glance at Old Cahawba: Alabama's Early Capital* (Selma: Coffee Printing, 1961), n.p.

22. Walker, *Cahaba Prison*, 4; Register, 377; Berry, *Loss of the Sultana*, 349–51.

23. Berry, *Loss of the Sultana*, 149; Charles King, "Boys of the War Days," in *The Photographic History of the Civil War*, Frances Trevelyan Miller, ed., 8:190.

24. Hawes, *Cahaba*, 126–51.

25. "Adventures of Geo. A. Tod, an Iowa Drummer Boy in Rebel Prisons at Cahawba and Andersonville," *Iowa Journal of History* 49 (1951): 342–43; Aldrich, *Cahawba Prison*, 8; Linda Derry, interview, October 5, 1986.

26. "Adventures of Geo. A. Tod," 343.

27. Berry, *Loss of the Sultana*, 298–300.

28. Ibid., 350; Walker, *Cahaba Prison*, 5; Hawes, *Cahaba*, 212; Aldrich, *Cahawba Prison*, 3, 5.

29. Hawes, *Cahaba*, 210.

30. Aldrich, *Cahawba Prison*, 2–3.

31. "Adventures of Geo A. Tod," 339–42.

32. *OR*, Ser. 2, 7:895–96.

33. Ibid., 1176–77, 1205; Henderson, "Lincoln's Assassination and Camp Fisk," 170.

34. Ibid.

5. The Hospital and the Toll

1. Fry, *Memories*, 25–26; Charles B. Reed, *The Curse of Cahawba* (Chicago: Pascal Covici, 1925), 35; *OR*, Ser. 2, 7:999; Register, 407–20.

2. Profilet's military records, National Archives; *OR*, Ser. 2, 7:999; Holley, *A History of Medicine in Alabama*, 141; Register, 410, 412, 414, 416. The doctors are referred to as surgeons here be-

cause that is what they were called during the Civil War. Brooks, *Civil War Medicine*, 22, 50; Fry, "Life in Dallas County During the War," 220.

3. Peter A. Brannon, ed., "Original Interments at Cahaba Military Cemetery—Now Interred at Marietta National Cemetery," *Alabama Historical Quarterly*, 25, No. 1 (1963): 192–96; Linda Derry, interview, October 5, 1986.

4. Day, *The Story of the One Hundred and First Ohio Infantry*, 342; Brooks, *Civil War Medicine*, 6; Hesseltine, *Civil War Prisons*, 256n.

5. Aldrich, "Cahawba Prison," 243. This is the version printed in *Camp-Fire Sketches*, which is slightly different from the version Aldrich printed as *Cahawba Prison*.

6. Montgomery *Advertiser*, March 14, 1894; Thomas McAdory Owen, ed., *Transactions of the Alabama Historical Society, 1897–1898*, 2 (1898): 126–27.

7. *OR*, Ser. 2, 8:946–47.

8. Register, 398–99, 401–403. Translations of the Latin medical terms used in the hospital records are from Frank P. Foster, *An Illustrated Encyclopaedic Medical Dictionary* (New York: D. Appleton, 1890).

9. Roll of Honor No. XIV, General Order No. 7, Quartermaster General's Office, Washington, D.C., February 20, 1868.

10. Surgeon Profilet and the Roll of Honor gave his name as Simail; Marietta National Cemetery spells it Simarl.

11. *OR*, Ser. 2, 7:999.

12. Hawes, *Cahaba*, 265–67; Register, 383.

13. "Adventures of Geo. A. Tod," 343; Aldrich, *Cahawba Prison*, 5.

14. *OR*, Ser. 2, 8:608, 7:999.

15. Berry, *Loss of the Sultana*, 367; Register, 398.

16. Register, 375, 377, 381, 384–86, 388–90, 392–96. The surgeons mixed Federal and Confederate records in the same journal, although on separate pages. *OR*, Ser. 2, 8:619; Brooks, *Civil War Medicine*, 85.

17. Register, 398–99, 401–403; Roll of Honor No. XIV.

18. Register, 400.

19. Hesseltine, *Civil War Prisons*, 146–47.

20. Holley, *The History of Medicine in Alabama*, 139; *OR*, Ser. 2, 7:1177.

21. Berry, *Loss of the Sultana*, 350; Register, 377, 408.

22. Register, 375, 384; Aldrich, *Cahawba Prison*, 6.

23. Hawes, *Cahaba*, 253; Register, 384; Requisition dated January 1, 1864, in Profilet's military records, National Archives.

24. *OR*, Ser. 2, 7:999; Register, 407–20; Hoole, ed., "The Battle of Athens and Letters from Cahawba Prison, 1864–1865," 151.

25. Register, 416, 418.

26. Ibid., 403.

27. Linda Derry, interview, October 5, 1986; Brannon, ed., "Original Interments at Cahaba Military Cemetery—Now Interred at Marietta National Cemetery," 196.

6. Amanda and Belle

1. Grigsby, *The Smoked Yank*, 75–88.

2. Deed Book T, 402, 765, Dallas County Courthouse, Selma; Grigsby, *The Smoked Yank*, 80; Hawes, *Cahaba*, 270; Linda Derry, interview, October 5, 1986.

3. Fry, *Memories*, 106; Census, Dallas County, 1860.

4. Deduced from the census records and the gravestone of the Gardners' first child. Cahaba had two cemeteries, one several hundred yards to the west, used in the earliest days, and a newer one at the southwest corner of town, which served in the final years. The Gardner girls were buried in the latter.

5. Deed Book T, 402, Dallas County Courthouse, Selma; Census, Dallas County, 1860.

6. U.S. Census, 1870, Dallas County.

7. Fry, *Memories*, 106.

8. Ibid., 104–106; *Brief Historical Sketches of Military Organizations Raised in Alabama During the Civil War*, The Alabama Civil War Centennial Commission, University, Alabama, 1962, 596–97.

9. Fry, 104–22; U.S. Census, 1860, Dallas County.

10. Grigsby, *The Smoked Yank*, 80; Deed Book T, 765, Dallas County Courthouse, Selma.

11. Grigsby, *The Smoked Yank*, 81.

12. Ibid., 83.

13. Futch, "Prison Life at Andersonville," 27–28.

14. Grigsby, *The Smoked Yank*, 82.

15. Ibid., 17, 38, 75.

16. Ibid., 76.

17. Ibid., 77.

18. Ibid., 80.

19. Hawes, *Cahaba*, 270–72.

20. Ibid., 274–75.

21. Ibid., 272–74; Grigsby, *The Smoked Yank*, 83.

22. Grigsby, *The Smoked Yank*, 81.

23. Hawes, *Cahaba*, 266–67.

24. Grigsby, *The Smoked Yank*, 83.

25. Ibid., 84, 85, 86; Hawes, *Cahaba*, 274.

26. Grigsby, *The Smoked Yank*, 85.

27. Ibid., 86–87.

28. Ibid., 87.

7. The Muggers and Big Tennessee

1. Jean P. Ray, *The Diary of a Dead Man, 1862–1864* (New York: Eastern Acorn Press, 1981), 246; Hawes, *Cahaba*, 219, 249, 250–51; Hesseltine, *Civil War Prisons*, 128, 145.

2. Military records of Private Richard M. Pierce, National Archives; Berry, *Loss of the Sultana*, 248.

3. Pierce military records, National Archives.

4. *Tennesseans in the Civil War*, Pt. 1 (Nashville: Tennessee Civil War Centennial Commission, 1964), 324, 325, 326.

5. Aldrich, *Cahawba Prison*, 1; Hoole, ed., "The Battle of Athens and Letters from Cahawba Prison, 1864–1865," 150–51.

6. The account of the fighting at Athens and Sulphur Trestle is taken from *OR*, Ser. 1, 39, Pt. 1:504–49. Among other accounts, see *Tennesseans in the Civil War*, Pt. 1:326; Steiner, *Disease in the Civil War*, 37.

7. Oliver P. Temple, *East Tennessee and the Civil War* (Cincinnati: Robert Clarke, 1899), 482; *OR*, Ser. 2, 8:803 passim.

8. Catton, "Prison Camps of the Civil War," 96; Randall and Donald, *The Civil War,* 329; *OR,* Ser. 3, 5:740–43; Ray, *The Diary of a Dead Man,* 246.

9. *OR,* Ser. 2, 7:426; Hesseltine, *Civil War Prisons,* 128, 144–45.

10. Hawes, *Cahaba,* 221, 222–27; Holley, *The History of Medicine in Alabama,* 139.

11. Hawes, *Cahaba,* 244.

12. Ibid., 246.

13. Fox, *Regimental Losses,* 62n; *Harper's Weekly,* August 19, 1865, p. 14.

14. Hawes, *Cahaba,* 247–48.

15. Ibid., 248.

16. Ibid., 251.

17. Berry, *Loss of the Sultana,* 248.

18. Ibid., 250.

19. Ibid., 249–51.

20. Memphis *Daily Bulletin,* April 28, 1865; Patricia M. La-Pointe, "Military Hospitals in Memphis, 1861–1865," *Tennessee Historical Quarterly,* 42, No. 4 (1983): 325–42; Pierce military records, National Archives.

8. Mutiny, Flood, Freedom

1. Henderson, "Lincoln's Assassination and Camp Fisk," 170; Aldrich, *Cahawba Prison,* 6, 7.

2. Aldrich, "Cahawba Prison" in *Camp-Fire Sketches,* 243.

3. *OR,* Ser. 2, 8:117–19.

4. Hawes, *Cahaba,* 383, 389.

5. Ibid., 386–89.

6. *OR,* Ser. 2, 7:1000.

7. Hawes, *Cahaba,* 404.

8. Ibid., 381–431; Walker, *Cahaba Prison,* 12; *OR,* Ser. 2, 8:117–22.

9. Berry, *Loss of the Sultana,* 144, 304, 324, 351; Hawes, *Cahaba,* 429; Walker, *Cahaba Prison,* 14.

10. *OR,* Ser. 2, 8:117–18.

11. Ibid., 118.

12. Ibid., 122.

13. Ibid.

14. Ibid., 467.

15. Ibid., 794–95, 834–35.

16. Hawes, *Cahaba*, 445; Berry, *Loss of the Sultana*, 262; Walker, *Cahaba Prison*, 14.

17. Hawes, *Cahaba*, 445, 446.

18. Aldrich, *Cahawba Prison*, 6; Walker, *Cahaba Prison*, 14–15.

19. Hawes, *Cahaba*, 453; Walker, *Cahaba Prison*, 14.

20. Hawes, *Cahaba*, 454; Berry, *Loss of the Sultana*, 352.

21. Hawes, *Cahaba*, 450, 451.

22. Kate Cumming, *A Journal of Hospital Life in the Confederate Army of Tennessee* (Louisville, Ky.: John P. Morton, 1866), 167.

23. *OR*, Ser. 2, 8:172–73.

24. Ibid., 98, 404.

25. Henderson, "Lincoln's Assassination and Camp Fisk," 170.

26. *OR*, Ser. 2, 8:404–405; Henderson, "Lincoln's Assassination and Camp Fisk," 170–71.

27. Berry, *Loss of the Sultana*, 262, 275, 352 passim.

28. Hawes, *Cahaba*, 458.

29. *The Tennessee Civil War Veterans Questionnaires*, 3 vols. (Easley, S.C.: Southern Historical Press, 1985), 1:154; Berry, *Loss of the Sultana*, 262.

30. Berry, *Loss of the Sultana*, 300.

31. Ibid., 29; Register, 416–18.

32. *OR*, Ser. 2, 8:437.

33. Ibid., 492–93.

34. Elliott, *Transport to Disaster*, 4.

9. The *Sultana*

1. Wilson M. Yager, "The Sultana Disaster," *Tennessee Historical Quarterly*, 35 (Spring–Winter 1976): 314; Elliott, *Transport to Disaster*, 92.

2. Cedric A. Larson, "Death on the Dark River," *American*

Heritage, 6 (October 1955): 50; Berry, *Loss of the Sultana*, 8. Other estimates vary. James Cornell, *The Great International Disaster Book* (New York: Charles Scribner's Sons, 1976), 319, gives the figure as 2,300 to 2,500 soldiers, plus 75 to 100 civilians and a crew of 80. Elliott, *Transport to Disaster*, 83–84.

3. Elliott, *Transport to Disaster*, 7–8; Berry, *Loss of the Sultana*, 25; New Orleans *Picayune*, April 19, 1865.

4. New Orleans *Picayune*, April 19, 1865, p. 7.

5. Elliott, *Transport to Disaster*, 32–33.

6. Frederick Way, Jr., *Way's Packet Directory, 1848–1983* (Athens: Ohio University Press, 1983), 436; Yager, "The Sultana Disaster," 309; Elliott, *Transport to Disaster*, 12.

7. Way, *Way's Packet Directory*, 436.

8. Elliott, *Transport to Disaster*, 14–16.

9. Ibid., 18; Yager, "The Sultana Disaster," 309.

10. Elliott, *Transport to Disaster*, 18–19.

11. *Official Records of the Union and Confederate Navies in the War of the Rebellion*, Ser. 1, 24:332–37, 420–21, 426–27, 546.

12. Elliott, *Transport to Disaster*, 19.

13. Ibid., 32–33.

14. Ray Samuel, Leonard V. Huber, and Warren C. Ogden, *Tales of the Mississippi* (New York: Hastings House, 1955), 31.

15. Elliott, *Transport to Disaster*, 16, 17; Leonard V. Huber, "Heyday of the Floating Palace," *American Heritage*, 8, No. 6 (October 1957), 23.

16. Way, *Way's Packet Directory*, 436; Elliott, *Transport to Disaster*, 33–34.

17. Elliott, *Transport to Disaster*, 42–44.

18. Ibid., 49–52.

19. Yager, "The Sultana Disaster," 308.

20. Elliott, *Transport to Disaster*, 56; Frank R. Levstik, "The Sinking of the Sultana," *Civil War Times Illustrated* (January 1974): 18–25; Yager, "The Sultana Disaster," 308.

21. Yager, "The Sultana Disaster," 310.

22. Elliott, *Transport to Disaster*, 74.

23. Levstik, "The Sinking of the Sultana," 21; Yager, "The Sultana Disaster," 307.

24. Berry, *Loss of the Sultana*, 383–419; Register, 374–96, 398–

403, 407–20; Steiner, *Disease in the Civil War*, 37; Roll of Honor No. XIV; *Tennesseans in the Civil War*, 326.

25. Way, *Way's Packet Directory*, 436.

26. Ibid., 436; Yager, "The Sultana Disaster," 314.

27. Memphis *Press-Scimitar*, June 7, 1983.

28. Berry, *Loss of the Sultana*, 29–31.

29. Ibid., 31–32.

30. *The Tennessee Civil War Veterans Questionnaires*, 1:143–46.

31. Berry, *Loss of the Sultana*, 10.

32. Ibid., 50, 51.

33. Ibid., 254–57.

34. Ibid., 349–54.

35. Ibid., 299–302.

36. Walker, *Cahaba Prison*, 19.

37. Ibid., 20–23.

38. Berry, *Loss of the Sultana*, 150.

39. Ibid., 149–52.

40. Ibid., 330–32.

41. Elliott, *Transport to Disaster*, 170–75.

42. Levstik, "The Sinking of the Sultana," 22.

43. Berry, *Loss of the Sultana*, 51–52.

44. LaPointe, "Military Hospitals in Memphis, 1861–1865," 325–42.

45. Hoole, ed., "The Battle of Athens and Letters from Cahawba Prison, 1864–1865," 153; Berry, *Loss of the Sultana*, 25.

46. *OR*, Ser. 1, Pt. 1:217; Way, *Way's Packet Directory*, 436.

10. Call Loud the Muster Roll

1. Yager, "The Sultana Disaster," 319–20.

2. Memphis *Argus*, April 28, 1865; New York *Times*, April 29, May 3, 1865; New York *Herald*, April 29–May 7, 1865.

3. Memphis *Daily Bulletin*, April 28, 1865; *Harper's Weekly*, May 13, 1865.

4. *Harper's Weekly*, May 20, 1865, p. 8.

5. *OR*, Ser. 1, 48, Pt. 1:217–20.

6. Berry, *Loss of the Sultana*, 25–26.

7. Ibid., 12–13.

8. Temple, *East Tennessee and the Civil War*, 483–84.

9. Register, 405, 418.

10. *OR*, Ser. 2, 8:951.

11. Ibid., Ser. 1, 59, Pt. 2:1273–90.

12. Jones's military records, National Archives.

13. *OR*, Ser. 2, 8:951.

14. Henderson, "Lincoln's Assassination and Camp Fisk," 170–71.

15. *OR*, Ser. 2, 8:498n.

16. Demopolis *New Era*, September 12, October 3, 1866. The only copies of the *New Era* found by the author to exist are in Birmingham, Alabama, public library.

17. Hawes, *Cahaba*, 256.

18. Lewis Collins, *History of Kentucky* (Covington: Collins & Co., 1878), 216; *History of Education in Kentucky*, 119, 120, 132.

19. Henderson, "Lincoln's Assassination and Camp Fisk," 171.

20. *History of Education in Kentucky*, 120.

21. Henderson's military records, National Archives; *Confederate Veteran*, 20 (March 1912): 126.

22. *History of Education in Kentucky*, 119–35.

23. Walker, *Cahaba Prison*, 1; Berry, *Loss of the Sultana*, 56, 149, 302, 369.

24. Grigsby, *The Smoked Yank*, 15; "Adventures of Geo. A. Tod," 339.

25. Yager, "The Sultana Disaster," 395; Associated Press article in the Montgomery *Advertiser*, May 9, 1988.

26. Reed, *The Curse of Cahawba*, 54–57.

Bibliography

Unpublished Primary Sources

Craig Family Papers. Provided by Dr. John M. Jackson, Eufaula, Alabama.

Dallas County Courthouse, Selma, Alabama. Deed Book AA, p. 481.

———. Deed Book KK, p. 214.

———. Deed Book S, p. 724.

———. Deed Book T, pp. 240, 400.

Derry, Linda. Archaeologist, Cahaba, Alabama. Interview, October 5, 1986.

Doorenbos, Dr. Norman J., Auburn University. Interviews on Civil War medicine, September 1988.

DuBose, John Witherspoon. "Chronicles of the Canebrake." Manuscript in the Alabama State Archives, Montgomery.

Henderson, H. A. M. Letter in Correspondence of Robert McKee. Alabama State Archives, Montgomery.

Marietta National Cemetery, Marietta, Georgia.

National Archives, Washington, D.C. "Deaths Among Federals" at Confederate Prison Hospital, Cahaba, Alabama. Record Group 249.

———. Military records of Lieutenant Colonel H. A. M. Henderson.

———. Military records of Lieutenant Colonel Sam Jones, Twenty-second Louisiana Volunteer Infantry.

———. Military records of Private Richard M. Pierce, Third Tennessee Cavalry.

———. Military records of Surgeon Louis E. Profilet.

———. Register of Federal Prisoners of War at Confederate Prison Hospital, Cahaba, Alabama. Record Group 249.

Oakley, Dr. Melvin L., Eufaula, Alabama. Analysis of hospital records, July 1987.

U.S. Census. Dallas County, Alabama, 1840.

———. Dallas County, Alabama, 1850.

———. Dallas County, Alabama, 1860.

———. Dallas County, Alabama, 1870.

Published Primary Sources

"Adventures of Geo. A. Tod, an Iowa Drummer Boy in Rebel Prisons at Cahawba and Andersonville." *Iowa Journal of History* (1951).

Aldrich, Hosea C. *Cahawba Prison: A Glimpse of Life in a Rebel Prison.* N.p., n.d.

———. "Cahawba Prison, Alabama." *Camp-Fire Sketches and Battle-Field Echoes of the Rebellion by "The Boys."* Springfield, 1887. N.p., n.d.

Beers, Henry Putney. *Guide to the Archives of the Government of the Confederate States of America.* Washington, D.C.: National Archives Publication No. 68–15, 1968.

Berry, Chester D. *Loss of the Sultana and Reminiscences of Survivors.* Lansing, Mich.: Darius D. Thorp, 1892.

Brannon, Peter A., ed. "Original Interments at Cahaba Military Cemetery—Now Interred at the Marietta National Cemetery." *Alabama Historical Quarterly,* 25, nos. 1–2 (1963).

Confederate Veteran, 20 (March 1912).

Cumming, Kate. *A Journal of Hospital Life in the Confederate Army of Tennessee.* Louisville, Ky.: John P. Morton & Co., 1866.

Day, Lewis W. *The Story of the One Hundred and First Ohio Infantry.* Cleveland, Ohio: W. M. Bayne Printing Co., 1894.

Fry, Anna M. Gayle. "Life in Dallas County During the War." *Confederate Veteran,* 24 (May 1916).

———. *Memories of Old Cahaba.* Nashville: Publishing House of the Methodist Episcopal Church, South, 1908.

Grigsby, Melvin. *The Smoked Yank.* Sioux Falls: Dakota Bell Publishing Co., 1888.

Harwell, J. D. "In and Around Vicksburg." *Confederate Veteran,* 30 (September 1922).

Hawes, Jesse. *Cahaba: A Story of Captive Boys in Blue.* New York: Burr Printing House, 1888.

Henderson, Howard A. M. "Lincoln's Assassination and Camp Fisk." *Confederate Veteran,* 15 (April 1907).

Hoole, William Stanley, ed. "The Battle of Athens and Letters from Cahawba Prison, 1864–1865." *Alabama Review,* 15 (January 1962).

Lossing, Benson J. *Pictorial History of the Civil War in the United States of America,* vol. 3. Hartford, 1877.

Miller, Francis Trevelyan, ed. *The Photographic History of the Civil War.* 10 vols. New York: Thomas Yoseloff, 1957.

Official Records of the Union and Confederate Navies in the War of the Rebellion. Washington, D.C.: Government Printing Office, 1894.

Records of Louisiana Confederate Soldiers and Louisiana Confederate Commands. 3 vols. Spartanburg, S.C.: Reprint Company, 1984.

Roll of Honor No. XIV, General Order No. 7, Quartermaster General's Office, Washington, D.C., February 20, 1868.

Ryan, Edmund E. Diary in the Peoria Historical Society, Peoria, Illinois.

The Official Military Atlas Of the Civil War. New York: The Fairfax Press, 1983.

The Tennessee Civil War Veterans Questionnaires. 3 vols. Easley, S.C.: Southern Historical Press, 1985.

The War of the Rebellion: A Compilation of the Official Records of the

Union and Confederate Armies. 130 vols. Washington, D.C.: Government Printing Office.

Walker, John L. *Cahaba Prison and the Sultana Disaster.* Hamilton, Ohio: Brown & Whitaker, 1910.

West, Emmet C. *History and Reminiscences of the Second Wisconsin Cavalry Regiment.* Portage, Wis.: State Register Print, 1914.

Newspapers

Demopolis *New Era,* August–October 1866.

Harper's Weekly, May 13, 20, August 19, 1865.

Memphis *Argus,* April 28, 1865.

Memphis *Daily Bulletin,* April 28, 1865.

Memphis *Press-Scimitar,* June 7, 1983.

Montgomery *Advertiser,* March 14, 1894.

Montgomery *Advertiser.* Associated Press article. May 9, 1988.

New Orleans *Picayune,* April 19, 20, 1865.

New York *Herald,* April 29–May 7, 1865.

New York *Times,* April 29–May 7, 1865.

Selma *Morning Reporter,* March 29, April 2, 11, May 13, 1864.

Secondary Sources

Armstrong, William M. "Cahaba to Charleston: The Prison Odyssey of Lt. Edmund E. Ryan." *Civil War History* (June 1962).

Black, Robert C. III. *The Railroads of the Confederacy.* Chapel Hill: University of North Carolina Press, 1952.

Brannon, Peter A. "The Cahawba Military Prison, 1863–1865." *Alabama Review* (July 1950).

Brantley, William H. *Three Capitals: A Book about the First Three Capitals of Alabama, St. Stephens, Huntsville, & Cahawba.* 1947; reprint ed., University: University of Alabama Press, 1976.

Brewer, W. *Alabama: Her History, Resources, War Record, and Public Men.* Montgomery: Barrett & Brown, 1872.

Brief Historical Sketches of Military Organizations Raised in Alabama

During the Civil War. Alabama Civil War Centennial Commission. University of Alabama, 1962.

Brooks, Stewart. *Civil War Medicine*. Springfield, Ohio: Charles C. Thomas, 1966.

Carter, Hodding. *Lower Mississippi*. New York: Farrar & Rinehart, 1942.

Catton, Bruce. "Prison Camps of the Civil War." *American Heritage* (August 1959).

Collins, Lewis. *History of Kentucky*. Covington, Ky.: Collins & Co., 1878.

Conrad, James L. "Held Captive at Cahaba." *Civil War Times Illustrated* (November 1982).

Cornell, James. *The Great International Disaster Book*. New York: Charles Scribner's Sons, 1976.

Coulter, Frederick Lee. "Years of Crisis, 1860–1870." *Memphis, 1800–1900*. New York: Nancy Powers & Company, 1982.

Elliott, James. *Transport to Disaster*. New York: Holt, Rinehart & Winston, 1962.

Foster, Frank P. *An Illustrated Encyclopaedic Medical Dictionary*. D. Appleton and Company, 1890.

Fox, William F. *Regimental Losses in the American Civil War*. Albany: Albany Publishing Company, 1889.

Freeman, Douglas Southall. *R. E. Lee: A Biography*. 4 vols. New York: Charles Scribner's Sons, 1936.

Futch, Ovid. "Prison Life at Andersonville." In *Civil War Prisons*, ed. William B. Hesseltine. Kent, Ohio: Kent State University Press, 1962.

Hesseltine, William Best. *Civil War Prisons: A Study in War Psychology*. Columbus: Ohio State University Press, 1930.

History of Education in Kentucky. Frankfort: Kentucky Department of Education, 1914.

Holley, Howard L. *The History of Medicine in Alabama*. Birmingham: University of Alabama School of Medicine, 1982.

Huber, Leonard V. "Heyday of the Floating Palace." *American Heritage* (October 1957).

Jackson, Walter M. *The Story of Selma*. Birmingham: Birmingham Printing Company, 1954.

LaPointe, Patricia M. "Military Hospitals in Memphis, 1861–1865." *Tennessee Historical Quarterly*, 42, No. 4 (1983).

Larson, Cedric A. "Death on the Dark River." *American Heritage*, 6 (October 1955).

Levstik, Frank R. "The Sinking of the Sultana." *Civil War Times Illustrated* (January 1974).

Livermore, Thomas L. *Numbers and Losses in the Civil War in America, 1861–65*. Boston: Houghton, Mifflin, 1901.

McDonough, James Lee, and James Picket Jones. *War So Terrible*. New York: W. W. Norton, 1987.

McMillan, Malcolm C. *The Alabama Confederate Reader*. Tuscaloosa: University of Alabama Press, 1963.

Neville, Bert. *A Glance at Old Cahawba: Alabama's Early Capital*. Selma: Coffee Printing Co., 1961.

Newby, I. A. *The South: A History*. New York: Holt, Rinehart & Winston, 1978.

Owen, Thomas McAdory, ed. *Transactions of the Alabama Historical Society, 1897–1898*, 2 (1898).

Randall, J. G., and David Herbert Donald. *The Civil War and Reconstruction*. Lexington, Mass.: D. C. Heath, 1969.

Ray, Jean P. *The Diary of a Dead Man, 1862–1864*. New York: Eastern Acorn Press, 1981.

Reed, Charles B. *The Curse of Cahawba*. Chicago: Pascal Covici, Publisher, 1925.

Rivers of Alabama. Huntsville: Strode Publishers, 1968.

Ross, Ishbel. *The General's Wife*. New York: Dodd, Mead & Company, 1959.

Samuel, Ray, Leonard V. Huber, and Warren C. Ogden. *Tales of the Mississippi*. New York: Hastings House, 1955.

Saxon, Lyle. *Father Mississippi*. New York: Century Company, 1927.

Steiner, Paul E. *Disease in the Civil War*. Springfield, Ohio: Charles C. Thomas, 1968.

Temple, Oliver P. *East Tennessee and the Civil War*. Cincinnati: Robert Clarke Co., 1899.

Tennesseans in the Civil War. Nashville: Tennessee Civil War Centennial Commission, 1964.

Way, Frederick, Jr. *Way's Packet Directory, 1848–1983*. Athens: Ohio University Press, 1983.

Yager, Wilson M. "The Sultana Disaster." *Tennessee Historical Quarterly*, 35 (Spring–Winter 1976).

Index

175

Index 177

Index   179